On BASE!

The Step-By-Step
Self-Esteem Program for
Children From Birth to 18

Barb Friedmann
Cheri Brooks

Editors

BASE Systems Publishers,
a division of Westport Publishers, Inc.
Kansas City, Missouri

Cover and text design by:
Noelle M. Kaplan, finedesign

Printed in the United States of America

ISBN 0-933701-43-8

Library of Congress Catalog Card Number:
89-40569

BASE and
are registered
in the U.S. Patent and Trademark Office.

Contents

Contents

Contents

Developers of **BASE**

Preface

While participating as community volunteers with our county social service department, we realized that there was a recurring theme that linked children who are considered high risk and suffer from the most glaring problems in our society—child abuse, domestic violence, drug abuse, suicide, etc.

They lacked good self-esteem!

The more issues we studied and the more professionals we talked with, the clearer it became that the answer to an independent, constructive, secure, and productive life is good self-esteem. This, in itself, is the greatest gift a parent can give a child; a teacher can give a student; a friend can give a friend.

If the lack of self-esteem can cause the ills of our society to take control of our lives, then the presence of good self-esteem can be the foundation on which a person can build a life of meaning and strength.

Self-esteem is the strength, the armor within needed to protect and guide us as our lives take direction.

Our idea was to design a program constructed on basic principles of self-esteem that would be easy to use and easy to understand.

We wanted to offer adults who interact with children on a consistent basis a tool that would achieve positive focused communication.

Living in Kansas City is a great advantage as we were able to utilize experts in two states, Kansas and Missouri. We interviewed over 200 professionals in the fields of pediatrics, social work, psychology, psychiatry, and education.

As the idea took shape into a workable plan, BASE (Behavioral Alternatives Through Self-Esteem) was born. Twelve of the professionals we had interviewed were asked to participate on a panel. This BASE Panel met regularly for over a year to develop and write the program exercise by exercise. An additional group of twenty-four experts offered their services and knowledge as members of the BASE Advisory Board. They played an active role by reviewing and approving all the material after each Panel meeting and by offering their own input in areas relative to their expertise. These people were some of the busiest people in our community; people who were concerned about making life better; people who care deeply about people; and most important to us, people who agreed that self-esteem is the essential element in the healthy growth and development of a child.

We found ourselves surrounded by 'believers.' The Johnson County (Kansas) Coalition for the Prevention of Child Abuse served as our organizational umbrella and administrative arm. Jeanetta Issa, their Executive Director, was a thoughtful guide and much appreciated friend. The Coalition board gave us the needed freedom to be creative and productive.

Our funders shared a faith in a positive program and in our plan for getting it done:

- Terry Ward with H & R Block Foundation;
- David Ross with Boatmen's Bank (John and Effie E. Speas Foundation);
- Dalene Bradford with The Greater Kansas City Foundation and Affiliated Trusts (George A. and Dolly F. LaRue Trust);
- Wendy Burcham with the Hall Family Foundation;
- Marshall Chatfield with Kansas City Life Insurance Company;
- Jan Armstrong with Kansas City Southern Industries;
- Nancy Yoffie with Payless Cashways, Inc.;
- Peggy Chism with J.C. Penney Company;
- Marjorie Powell Allen with the Powell Family Foundation;
- Candace Fowler, Oppenstein Brothers Foundation

Preface

Not only did they supply the needed funding, they supplied ideas, constructive suggestions, and support for every stage of BASE development. They bolstered our self-esteem by believing in an idea and by believing in us.

Many agencies and groups through child care professionals or related parties have utilized BASE on an ongoing basis:

- Division of Family Services, Jackson County, MO
- Social Rehabilitation Services, Johnson County, KS
- Argentine Kansas Youth Services
- Wyandotte County Community Corrections
- U.S. Army Hospital, Ft. Leavenworth, KS
- Heart of America Indian Center
- Center School District, Kansas City, MO—Missouri Parents as Teachers
- Spofford Residential Center for Children
- Missouri Department of Corrections
- Farm Assistance Council Training Service in Rural Kansas
- NEWS, A Battered Women's Shelter and Day Care Facility
- University of Kansas Medical Center in staff training and in the Children's Rehabilitation Unit.

BASE is participating in a current pilot of the Independence, Missouri School District involving child care (3-12 year olds, full day, before and after school) and regular classroom instruction.

BASE is participating in a current pilot with the YWCA in the Kansas City metro area involving infant care, 2-5 year day care, Y Land Camps (5-14 years of age), Latchkey Program, Mother's Center, Summer Youth Employment, Career Development, Teen Mothers' Center, Between Us Girls (BUG), Babysitting Clinics, and Young Women's Mentor Program.

We were acknowledged as a 1988 recipient of J.C. Penney's Golden Rule Award for the development of BASE. We also received the Johnson County Coalition for the Prevention of Child Abuse Recognition Award for an Outstanding Contribution in the Prevention of Child Abuse.

BASE has been presented in workshop form at the Kansas City, Missouri Mayor's Conference on Youth Development; in Anaheim California, the National Symposium of Child Victimization; and as a Technical Forum at the Eighth National Conference on Child Abuse and Neglect in Salt Lake City, Utah.

We thank Dr. Arnold Moskowitz and Adele B. Levi for their guidance and resourcefulness. Many thanks to our director and guide; our editor and friend, Terry Faulkner with whom it is a pleasure sharing a creative vision.

Special gratitude and appreciation goes to our families whose unwavering support and encouragement has been our strength. They have shared our excitement, our concern, our anxiety, and our pride.

B.F.
C.B.

Introduction

BASE (Behavioral Alternatives Through Self-Esteem)® is a system of focusing consistent, positive attention on a child. It gives direction and purpose to a communication or activity that is shared between a child and a care-giver. It offers a *reason* to interact. What makes this interaction unique is that it is built on key components of self-esteem.

Self-esteem is the way we relate to ourselves, to others, and to life. It affects the way we learn, work, and build relationships. It is what we believe about ourselves.

If we believe we **can**...we **do!**

If we believe we **can't**...we **don't even try!**

Our success or failure lies in the foundation of self-esteem that we carry within us. Many components come together to assure the strength of that foundation. Those components and the way they are communicated are what the BASE Program is all about.

BASE offers a means of communication between a child and those who share their life with that child.

This communication springs not from common sense, that differs with the experience of each individual, but from the basic elements of self-esteem that can literally create a *base* for the child.

BASE is a series of user friendly exercises and communications, written at a basic primary skill/vocabulary level, that can be implemented within 30 seconds to three minutes per activity.

BASE was created by professionals in pediatrics, psychology, education, psychiatry, child development, social work and related social services.

BASE was professionally evaluated by the Department of Human Development at the University of Kansas under the guidance of Kathryn Kirigin Ramp, Ph.D. and by Elizabeth Noble, Ph.D., Director of Family Study Center at the University of Missouri-Kansas City.

❑ *Self-esteem Building Blocks*

The activities and communications developed for BASE are constructed on core building blocks of self-esteem. Please note that the definitions of these terms may not be traditional dictionary definitions; instead, they "speak to" certain needs in all of us.

❑ *Approval*

Demonstrated recognition which complements something the child has done or initiated (approval of effort is often as valuable as approval of accomplishment).

❑ *Trust*

Expression of belief in another's (the child's) honesty. Expression of confidence in the child's sense of maturity or responsibility.

❑ *Sense of Power*

Knowing that "in this arena", one has superior skills, or (at least) skills equal to anyone else in the same arena. Feeling the collective strength of those with whom one is associated at a given time (a good team, club, gang, etc.).

❑ *Acceptance*

One's feeling that others appreciate who he or she is, based on *What* is rather than *Who* one is (i.e., acceptance/approval of one's character).

❑ *Responsibility*

The knowledge that one can accept—and that others expect one to accept—duties, morals, and commitments, and, without unnecessary persuasion, accomplishes tasks and behaves "properly".

❑ *Self-respect*

Internalizes the assurance that one is living up to personal standards and self-expectations (of achievement, morality, trust) to the best of one's ability.

Introduction

☐ *Respect for Others*
Displaying an appreciation for the "personhood" of others without regard for fashion, status or ability, but with regard to the fact that we share mortality and fallibility.

☐ *Flexibility*
The ability to hold to standards with steadfastness and discipline, and yet without rigidity. The ability to assess one's surroundings and make appropriate adjustments in thought and behavior.

☐ *Pride*
Feeling good about one's self, often because of some accomplishment recognized by respected others.

☐ *Sense of Importance*
Feeling that others regard one as a significant contributor to the human experience—even if recognized for "small" tasks and achievements.

The BASE program is divided into 15 developmental levels that range between birth and 18 years:

Level 1: 0-3 months	**Level 9:** 1st-2nd grade
Level 2: 3-9 months	**Level 10:** 3rd-4th grade
Level 3: 9-15 months	**Level 11:** 5th-6th grade
Level 4: 15-24 months	**Level 12:** 7th-8th grade
Level 5: 2-3 years	**Level 13:** 9th grade
Level 6: 3-4 years	**Level 14:** 10th grade
Level 7: 4-5 years	**Level 15:** 11th-12th grade
Level 8: 5 yrs-Kindergarten	

• Each level offers a listing of characteristics (behavioral and growth) for that given level.
• A general information page is given to acquaint others to the program.

• Human awareness information is included in levels 5 through 15 and covers special topics relative to the level of the child, with suggested communications for the adults interacting with the child (i.e., friendships, drugs, sex, communicating, relationships, what's "normal", etc.).
• All the exercises, activities, and communications can involve up to four people who are consistent in the life of the child (i.e., parent, teacher, day care provider, relative, neighbor, or friend).
• The exercises are written at a basic primary vocabulary/skill level and are presented in a step-by-step format.

BASE is a way of urging and supporting those involved in the life of a child to play a **direct role** in helping to encourage positive reinforcement and growth...good self-esteem!

BASE encourages **communication** between **all** the "players" in the life of the child.

BASE is **child-centered**.

BASE creates a **positive** outcome, then reinforces it.

The goal is to heighten and develop understanding of **self-worth** in the child and by the mere communication of the exercise to do the same for the contributing adult involved.

BASE is not designed to take the place of any therapeutic services offered the child. It is designed to work in conjunction with those provided services to reinforce the positive self-worth of the individual.

The thrust of BASE is to integrate positive communications into the everyday life of the child.

Instructions

1. Exercise page for facilitators:
   The following capital letter appears at the top corner of each exercise page:
   A — for **Parent (Custodial Parent)/ Primary Care Provider**
   B — for **Parent** (only needed in case of separation or divorce/for parent living away from the primary home of the child)
   C — for **Day Care Provider/ Babysitter/Teacher**
   D — for interacting **Relative** or **Friend** (i.e., grandparent, neighbor)
   ☐ — denotes Self-Esteem Building Blocks that were used to construct the communication or activity
   ● — denotes an exercise

2. Identify and locate the child's **Level**. This is done by the child's age or grade **plus** the developmental skills listed on the **Level Characteristics** page. The skills indicated are "average" for the particular age group. It will be most helpful if you look over the developmental skills on the level prior to the child's age and the next level beyond the child's age; then you can best decide which level the child should begin BASE. Remember, BASE is an individualized program which means that regardless of the age of the child, he or she begins BASE according to his or her individual skills and needs…emotionally, physically, and mentally.

3. After you've selected the **Level** best suited for the child:
   Read the **Information** page, special **Teacher Information** page (where available) and the **Human Awareness** page (where available).

4. Review all facilitator **Exercise** pages so that you are aware of the exercises that others will be using to interact with the child.

5. Assign the facilitator Exercise pages when appropriate:
   B — To parent, **not** the custodial parent, in case of separation or divorce. They should also review or get a copy of the **Information** page, and the **Human Awareness** page where available.
   C — To Day Care Provider/ Babysitter/Teacher.
   D — To a Relative or Friend (i.e., grandparent, aunt, uncle, neighbor, etc.).

6. Explain to each facilitator the intent of the BASE program, which simply put is to enhance or build a child's self-esteem. Review the importance of the Self-Esteem Building Blocks. Remember that BASE offers focused communication between the child and the adults in his or her life, and that BASE was designed to fit into the daily life and activities of the child and family…not to be separate from it.

7. Be **consistent**! Consistency gives structure and that takes time to build. It is a goal of BASE to offer a daily routine from which consistency grows.

8. Stress to each facilitator how important it is to **keep trying** and that they must have **patience** with themselves and with the child.

   Don't give up! These exercises may not work today or even tomorrow, but **keep trying!**

   (continued…)

Instructions

If you don't see progress immediately, it does not mean that you or that the child is a failure!

Nobody fails BASE!

9. Every exercise or activity may not be for every facilitator or every child. If the child is uncooperative towards doing an activity after consistent efforts on the part of the facilitator, **drop the activity** and continue with the ones that are working.

10. If you think you and your child are ready to move on to the next Level (beginning with Level 5 through Level 15), here are some clues to help you decide:
    a. Can the child do the exercises easily?
    b. Are you more positive with the child?
    c. Do you find the child more positive about himself or herself?
    d. Are you finding it easier to talk to the child about lots of different things?

    If the answer to the above four questions is "yes" look at the next Level.

    If you feel the child can do at least two new activities within that Level, move to that Level.

    If you find the child is not ready for these activities, don't move to the next Level.

Level 1 Characteristics

- Turns head side to side
- Smiles
- Has extended reach and grabs
- Makes fist 50% of the time
- Has head control while in prone position
- Coos
- Raises up on extended forearms
- Awaits food
- Reacts to a smile
- Seeks human sound source
- Follows people with eyes
- Explores body (example: hand to mouth)
- Imitates sounds

Level 1 Information

Self-esteem is a feeling.
If you have HIGH self-esteem…
    You make good friends!
    You care about yourself and other people;
    You are responsible;
    You enjoy learning;
    You are proud of what you do;
    You can handle failure;
    You can share feelings.

HIGH self-esteem is having a GOOD feeling about yourself, your place in the family, your school, and your world.

THINGS TO REMEMBER:
- No sudden jerky movements.
- No loud noises.
- Use a quiet "inside" voice.
- Have baby sleep on tummy.
- Show a "happy" face to the baby.
- SMILE every time you look at the baby.
- Think in a loving way toward the baby.
- Protect the baby.
- MOTHER'S TIME-OUT IS OK. You NEED time for yourself!
- NO baby talk!
- Always try to be CALM and SURE of yourself when you are around the baby.
- It is okay for a baby to be fussy…it is his or her way of telling you something.

DON'T GIVE UP!
— If the child does not want to do the activity with you the way you want him or her to…try again tomorrow.
— Keep trying. This is the way you **SHOW** the child that you mean what you say. A child needs to **TRUST** in order to share with you or listen to you.
— **HOW** you say something is sometimes more important than **WHAT** you say.

You may be doing MOST of these things already as part of the way you care for children and run your home. By doing these things in the way they are written, you will be helping the child's self-esteem **plus** your own self-esteem.

When you can help somebody feel good… you feel good!

The BASE program is about helping children have HIGH self-esteem. It is a group of things to do and share with a child. These things are short, simple and positive. They should be done everyday when possible.

REMEMBER:
If any of these things do not agree with the way you believe or your religion (example: dancing), do not do it.

❏ *Approval* ❏ *Trust*
● **THE WAY TO FEED
THE BABY WITH A BOTTLE.**
1. Go to a quiet place to feed the baby.
2. Hold bottle in the hand you use for writing. Hold baby in other arm…head resting at your elbow…body resting on the front part of your arm…your hand holding the baby's bottom…the baby resting on your waist.
3. Talk softly to the baby but do not use baby talk. The baby will hear the right way to talk. Talk to the baby about something and SMILE!
4. SMILE and look into the baby's eyes.
5. Sing songs to the baby like "Mary Had a Little Lamb" or "London Bridge"…or any song you like…the baby will like the sound.
6. Burp the baby. Hold baby with the head on your shoulder and the face close to your cheek. Pat the baby gently on the back until you hear the burp.

❏ *Trust* ❏ *Flexibility*
● **DIAPERING THE BABY.**
1. Make sure you have everything you need.
2. Gently put the baby down on the bed, floor, table, or wherever you will change the baby.
3. Give the baby something bright…and SAFE…to hold while being diapered.
4. Look into the baby's eyes. Get the baby to look at you. SMILE and talk to the baby.
5. Talk quietly or sing a song like "Twinkle, Twinkle Little Star" or "Old MacDonald Had a Farm".
6. Always touch the baby GENTLY when you change the diaper.
7. When the clean diaper is on the baby, pick up the baby. Be sure one hand is holding the baby's head.
8. Love the baby by putting the head on your shoulder with the face near your cheek and the body on your chest.

❏ *Trust*
● **YOU AND BABY TOGETHER (CAN BE DONE A FEW TIMES A DAY).**
1. Pick up baby and go to a quiet place.
2. Hold baby in your arms, head resting at your elbow. The baby's body will rest on the front part of your arm and your hand will hold the baby's bottom. The baby will rest on your waist.
3. Slowly rock the baby back and forth in your arms.

4. Look into the baby's eyes while you are rocking the baby.
5. Talk to the baby in a soft and gentle voice. Tell the baby about the things he or she is doing. You might say: "You are kicking your legs."…"You are making such a funny noise."…"You are having so much fun smiling." Tell the baby anything he or she is doing. DO NOT USE BABY TALK! (Use clear words.)
6. Tell the baby about things you see in the room. You may want to talk about the sound that a clock makes, or how soft a chair is when you sit down, or about a table in the room, or the things on the table.
7. Look into the baby's eyes and SMILE.
8. Sit down in a chair (if standing).
9. Hold the baby with your two hands on his or her body and under the arms and let baby try to stand on your lap. Let baby use his or her legs to push on your lap.
10. Tell baby that you are very proud of him or her. Use the baby's name. The baby will learn that he or she is doing something good.
11. Be sure to give the baby a gentle hug and kiss.

❏ *Trust*
● **THE WAY TO GIVE THE BABY A BATH.**
1. Get all the things you will need for the bath: towel, washcloth, soap, bath toy, powder, or anything else you need. Put them where the baby will have the bath. You can use a tub made for a baby's bath or maybe use the sink in the kitchen.
2. Make water as deep as your finger is long. Feel the water with your hand or elbow. Be sure that it's not too hot or too cold.
3. Put the baby down on the bed, floor, or table and take off all the clothes.
4. Talk to the baby. The baby will hear the sound of your voice and will learn from it.
5. Put the baby in the water on his or her back. Be sure to hold the head out of the water. Tell the baby how nice it is to have a bath. The baby will learn that a bath is a good thing by hearing the NICE WAY you are talking.
6. Be sure to hold the back of the baby's head all the time. Put soap on a soft washcloth. Wash the baby; being sure that you don't rub too hard. Wash baby all over…also hair.
7. When baby makes a noise, you make a noise back to the baby. If the baby moves his or her arms or legs to splash the water, you can play along with the baby. Make a bath a FUN time.
(continued…)

8. Take the baby out of the water, holding gently. Lay the baby on the towel and dry gently. Put on any powders or creams that you use on the baby.
9. Put a diaper on the baby. Dress the baby. Keep talking to baby and look into baby's eyes.
10. Pick up baby and give a BIG HUG!

❏ *Approval* ❏ *Acceptance*

● **PLAYING WITH THE BABY USING A BIG BRIGHT TOY.**

1. Put a blanket or something else that is soft on the floor. Then put the baby on his or her stomach on the blanket.
2. Now lay down on your stomach in front of the baby so your head will be near the baby's head.
3. Look at the baby and get the baby to look at you.
4. SMILE at the baby.
5. Talk to the baby the same way you would talk to anyone else. NO BABY TALK! (Use short sentences and talk clearly.)
6. Hold a ball or a bright toy. Move it from side to side in front of the baby's face so baby can see it. Then move it way off to the side where baby cannot see it, slowly moving it back to where baby can see it again.
7. Pat the baby gently on the back.
8. Hold toy closer to baby so baby can touch it.
9. Keep talking to baby. Keep SMILING!

❏ *Trust* ❏ *Flexibility*

● **THE RIGHT WAY TO GIVE OR HAND A BABY FROM YOU TO SOMEONE ELSE.**

1. This is something to do SLOWLY and CAREFULLY.
2. Hold the back part of the baby's head with one hand. Use your other hand to hold the baby's rear or bottom.
3. Stand close to the other person when you are ready to hand over the baby.
4. Hand the baby to the other person.
5. When you give the baby to the other person, smile and say the baby's name…using a nice soft voice.

❏ *Approval* ❏ *Trust*

● **THE WAY TO FEED
THE BABY WITH A BOTTLE.**

1. Go to a quiet place to feed the baby.
2. Hold bottle in the hand you use for writing. Hold baby in other arm…head resting at your elbow…body resting on the front part of your arm…your hand holding the baby's bottom…the baby resting on your waist.
3. Talk softly to the baby but do not use baby talk. The baby will hear the right way to talk. Talk to the baby about something and SMILE!
4. SMILE and look into the baby's eyes.
5. Sing songs to the baby like "Mary Had a Little Lamb" or "London Bridge"…or any song you like…the baby will like the sound.
6. Burp the baby. Hold baby with the head on your shoulder and the face close to your cheek. Pat the baby gently on the back until you hear the burp.

❏ *Trust* ❏ *Flexibility*

● **DIAPERING THE BABY.**

1. Make sure you have everything you need.
2. Gently put the baby down on the bed, floor, table, or wherever you will change the baby.
3. Give the baby something bright…and SAFE…to hold while being diapered.
4. Look into the baby's eyes. Get the baby to look at you. SMILE and talk to the baby.
5. Talk quietly or sing a song like "Twinkle, Twinkle Little Star" or "Old MacDonald Had a Farm".
6. Always touch the baby GENTLY when you change the diaper.
7. When the clean diaper is on the baby, pick up the baby. Be sure one hand is holding the baby's head.
8. Love the baby by putting the head on your shoulder with the face near your cheek and the body on your chest.

❏ *Trust*

● **YOU AND BABY TOGETHER (CAN BE DONE A FEW TIMES A DAY).**

1. Pick up baby and go to a quiet place.
2. Hold baby in your arms, head resting at your elbow. The baby's body will rest on the front part of your arm and your hand will hold the baby's bottom. The baby will rest on your waist.
3. Slowly rock the baby back and forth in your arms.

4. Look into the baby's eyes while you are rocking the baby.
5. Talk to the baby in a soft and gentle voice. Tell the baby about the things he or she is doing. You might say: "You are kicking your legs."…"You are making such a funny noise."…"You are having so much fun smiling." Tell the baby anything he or she is doing. DO NOT USE BABY TALK! (Use clear words.)
6. Tell the baby about things you see in the room. You may want to talk about the sound that a clock makes, or how soft a chair is when you sit down, or about a table in the room, or the things on the table.
7. Look into the baby's eyes and SMILE.
8. Sit down in a chair (if standing).
9. Hold the baby with your two hands on his or her body and under the arms and let baby try to stand on your lap. Let baby use his or her legs to push on your lap.
10. Tell baby that you are very proud of him or her. Use the baby's name. The baby will learn that he or she is doing something good.
11. Be sure to give the baby a gentle hug and kiss.

❏ *Trust*

● **THE WAY TO GIVE THE BABY A BATH.**

1. Get all the things you will need for the bath: towel, washcloth, soap, bath toy, powder, or anything else you need. Put them where the baby will have the bath. You can use a tub made for a baby's bath or maybe use the sink in the kitchen.
2. Make water as deep as your finger is long. Feel the water with your hand or elbow. Be sure that it's not too hot or too cold.
3. Put the baby down on the bed, floor, or table and take off all the clothes.
4. Talk to the baby. The baby will hear the sound of your voice and will learn from it.
5. Put the baby in the water on his or her back. Be sure to hold the head out of the water. Tell the baby how nice it is to have a bath. The baby will learn that a bath is a good thing by hearing the NICE WAY you are talking.
6. Be sure to hold the back of the baby's head all the time. Put soap on a soft washcloth. Wash the baby; being sure that you don't rub too hard. Wash baby all over…also hair.
7. When baby makes a noise, you make a noise back to the baby. If the baby moves his or her arms or legs to splash the water, you can

(continued…)

play along with the baby. Make a bath a FUN time.

8. Take the baby out of the water, holding gently. Lay the baby on the towel and dry gently. Put on any powders or creams that you use on the baby.

9. Put a diaper on the baby. Dress the baby. Keep talking to baby and look into baby's eyes.

10. Pick up baby and give a BIG HUG!

❏ *Approval* ❏ *Acceptance*

● **PLAY WITH BABY USING A BRIGHT TOY.**

1. Hold baby having the head rest at your elbow. The baby's body will be resting on the front part of your arm and your hand will hold the baby's bottom. The baby will rest on your waist.

2. Put a BIG BRIGHT toy in the hand you use for writing. Hold the baby in your other arm.

3. Look at the baby. Get the baby to look at you.

4. Hold the toy in front of the baby (about as far away as the size of your hand).

5. Move the toy back and forth...to the right of the baby's face a little way, then to the left a little way...then to the right again...then to the left again.

6. Repeat this three times. Watch baby's eyes follow the toy.

7. Now, hold the toy two hand sizes away from baby's face.

8. Move toy to the right...then to the left.

9. Repeat this three times.

10. Keep talking to baby, telling him or her how good he or she is.

❏ *Approval* ❏ *Acceptance*

● **PLAYING WITH THE BABY USING A BIG BRIGHT TOY.**

1. Put a blanket or something else that is soft on the floor. Then put the baby on his or her stomach on the blanket.

2. Now lay down on your stomach in front of the baby so your head will be near the baby's head.

3. Look at the baby and get the baby to look at you.

4. SMILE at the baby.

5. Talk to the baby the same way you would talk to anyone else. NO BABY TALK! (Use short sentences and talk clearly.)

6. Hold a ball or a bright toy. Move it from side to side in front of the baby's face so baby can see it. Then move it way off to the side where baby cannot see it, slowly moving it back to where baby can see it again.

7. Pat the baby gently on the back.

8. Hold toy closer to baby so baby can touch it.

9. Keep talking to baby. Keep SMILING!

❏ *Trust* ❏ *Flexibility*

● **THE RIGHT WAY TO GIVE OR HAND A BABY FROM YOU TO SOMEONE ELSE.**

1. This is something to do SLOWLY and CAREFULLY.

2. Hold the back part of the baby's head with one hand. Use your other hand to hold the baby's rear or bottom.

3. Stand close to the other person when you are ready to hand over the baby.

4. Hand the baby to the other person.

5. When you give the baby to the other person, smile and say the baby's name...using a nice soft voice.

❏ *Approval* ❏ *Trust*

● **THE WAY TO FEED THE BABY WITH A BOTTLE.**

1. Go to a quiet place to feed the baby.
2. Hold bottle in the hand you use for writing. Hold baby in other arm…head resting at your elbow…body resting on the front part of your arm…your hand holding the baby's bottom…the baby resting on your waist.
3. Talk softly to the baby but do not use baby talk. The baby will hear the right way to talk. Talk to the baby about something and SMILE!
4. SMILE and look into the baby's eyes.
5. Sing songs to the baby like "Mary Had a Little Lamb" or "London Bridge"…or any song you like…the baby will like the sound.
6. Burp the baby. Hold baby with the head on your shoulder and the face close to your cheek. Pat the baby gently on the back until you hear the burp.

❏ *Trust* ❏ *Flexibility*

● **DIAPERING THE BABY.**

1. Make sure you have everything you need.
2. Gently put the baby down on the bed, floor, table, or wherever you will change the baby.
3. Give the baby something bright…and SAFE…to hold while being diapered.
4. Look into the baby's eyes. Get the baby to look at you. SMILE and talk to the baby.
5. Talk quietly or sing a song like "Twinkle, Twinkle Little Star" or "Old MacDonald Had a Farm".
6. Always touch the baby GENTLY when you change the diaper.
7. When the clean diaper is on the baby, pick up the baby. Be sure one hand is holding the baby's head.
8. Love the baby by putting the head on your shoulder with the face near your cheek and the body on your chest.

❏ *Approval* ❏ *Acceptance*

● **PLAY WITH BABY USING A BRIGHT TOY.**

1. Hold baby having the head rest at your elbow. The baby's body will be resting on the front part of your arm and your hand will hold the baby's bottom. The baby will rest on your waist.
2. Put a BIG BRIGHT toy in the hand you use for writing. Hold the baby in your other arm.
3. Look at the baby. Get the baby to look at you.
4. Hold the toy in front of the baby (about as far away as the size of your hand).
5. Move the toy back and forth…to the right of the baby's face a little way, then to the left a little way…then to the right again…then to the left again.
6. Repeat this three times. Watch baby's eyes follow the toy.
7. Now, hold the toy two hand sizes away from baby's face.
8. Move toy to the right…then to the left.
9. Repeat this three times.
10. Keep talking to baby, telling him or her how good he or she is.

❏ *Trust* ❏ *Flexibility*

● **THE RIGHT WAY TO GIVE OR HAND A BABY FROM YOU TO SOMEONE ELSE.**

1. This is something to do SLOWLY and CAREFULLY.
2. Hold the back part of the baby's head with one hand. Use your other hand to hold the baby's rear or bottom.
3. Stand close to the other person when you are ready to hand over the baby.
4. Hand the baby to the other person.
5. When you give the baby to the other person, smile and say the baby's name…using a nice soft voice.

❒ *Trust*

● **YOU AND BABY TOGETHER (CAN BE DONE A FEW TIMES A DAY).**

1. Pick up baby and go to a quiet place.
2. Hold baby in your arms, head resting at your elbow. The baby's body will rest on the front part of your arm and your hand will hold the baby's bottom. The baby will rest on your waist.
3. Slowly rock the baby back and forth in your arms.
4. Look into the baby's eyes while you are rocking the baby.
5. Talk to the baby in a soft and gentle voice. Tell the baby about the things he or she is doing. You might say: "You are kicking your legs."..."You are making such a funny noise."..."You are having so much fun smiling." Tell the baby anything he or she is doing. DO NOT USE BABY TALK! (Use clear words.)
6. Tell the baby about things you see in the room. You may want to talk about the sound that a clock makes, or how soft a chair is when you sit down, or about a table in the room, or the things on the table.
7. Look into the baby's eyes and SMILE.
8. Sit down in a chair (if standing).
9. Hold the baby with your two hands on his or her body and under the arms and let baby try to stand on your lap. Let baby use his or her legs to push on your lap.
10. Tell baby that you are very proud of him or her. Use the baby's name. The baby will learn that he or she is doing something good.
11. Be sure to give the baby a gentle hug and kiss.

❒ *Approval* ❒ *Acceptance*

● **PLAY WITH BABY USING A BRIGHT TOY.**

1. Hold baby having the head rest at your elbow. The baby's body will be resting on the front part of your arm and your hand will hold the baby's bottom. The baby will rest on your waist.
2. Put a BIG BRIGHT toy in the hand you use for writing. Hold the baby in your other arm.
3. Look at the baby. Get the baby to look at you.
4. Hold the toy in front of the baby (about as far away as the size of your hand).
5. Move the toy back and forth...to the right of the baby's face a little way, then to the left a little way...then to the right again...then to the left again.
6. Repeat this three times. Watch baby's eyes follow the toy.
7. Now, hold the toy two hand sizes away from baby's face.
8. Move toy to the right...then to the left.
9. Repeat this three times.
10. Keep talking to baby, telling him or her how good he or she is.

❒ *Trust* ❒ *Flexibility*

● **THE RIGHT WAY TO GIVE OR HAND A BABY FROM YOU TO SOMEONE ELSE.**

1. This is something to do SLOWLY and CAREFULLY.
2. Hold the back part of the baby's head with one hand. Use your other hand to hold the baby's rear or bottom.
3. Stand close to the other person when you are ready to hand over the baby.
4. Hand the baby to the other person.
5. When you give the baby to the other person, smile and say the baby's name...using a nice soft voice.

Level 1

3-9 months

Level 2 Characteristics

- Laughs
- Hand can open fully
- Sits, straight back
- Plays with rattle
- Enjoys mirror
- Puts foot to mouth
- Makes sound like "Mama" and "Dada"
- Understands "No"
- Creeps
- Grabs
- Pulls up to stand
- Plays "pat-a-cake", "peek-a-boo"
- Babbles
- Inspects toys
- Wake/sleep schedule becoming regular
- Explores body (example: intertwining of fingers)

Level 2 Information

Self-esteem is a feeling.
If you have HIGH self-esteem…

>   You make good friends!
>   You care about yourself and other people;
>   You are responsible;
>   You enjoy learning;
>   You are proud of what you do;
>   You can handle failure;
>   You can share feelings.

HIGH self-esteem is having a GOOD feeling about yourself, your place in the family, your school, and your world.

THINGS TO REMEMBER:

- Speak in a soft, gentle voice.
- When the baby is good…tell him or her.
- Use the baby's name.
- It's okay for a baby to be "fussy." It is their way of telling you something.
- SMILE at the baby!
- NO BABY TALK! Talk to the baby the way you always talk.
- Use simple words to tell the baby what you want.
- SHOW, as well as TELL the baby what you want done.
- If the baby does not do things right the first time…it's okay.
- KEEP TRYING!
- LOOK for the Good Stuff!

DON'T GIVE UP!

- If the child does not want to do the activity with you the way you want him or her to…try again tomorrow.
- Keep trying. This is the way you **SHOW** the child that you mean what you say. A child needs to **TRUST** in order to share with you or listen to you.
- **HOW** you say something is sometimes more important than **WHAT** you say.

You may be doing MOST of these things already as part of the way you care for children and run your home. By doing these things in the way they are written, you will be helping the child's self-esteem **plus** your own self-esteem.

When you can help somebody feel good… you feel good!

The BASE program is about helping children have HIGH self-esteem. It is a group of things to do and share with a child. These things are short, simple and positive. They should be done everyday when possible.

REMEMBER:

If any of these things do not agree with the way you believe or your religion (example: dancing), do not do it.

❏ *Approval* ❏ *Trust*
● **THE WAY TO FEED THE BABY WITH A BOTTLE.**
1. Go to a quiet place to feed the baby.
2. Hold bottle in the hand you use for writing. Hold baby in other arm…head resting at your elbow…body resting on the front part of your arm…your hand holding the baby's bottom…the baby resting on your waist.
3. Talk softly to the baby but do not use baby talk. The baby will then hear the right way to talk. Talk to the baby about something and SMILE!
4. SMILE and look into baby's eyes.
5. Sing songs to the baby like "Mary Had a Little Lamb" or "London Bridge"…or any song you like…the baby will like the sound.
6. Baby may want to hold the bottle himself or herself. This is okay!
7. Burp the baby.

❏ *Approval* ❏ *Trust* ❏ *Sense of Power*
● **HERE ARE THINGS TO SAY TO THE BABY WHILE YOU PUT THE DIAPER ON. (Talk to the baby but do not ask questions. Talk softly, look happy, and use your hands gently when doing these things.)**
1. Hold the baby's hand. Tell the baby: "This is your hand."
2. Put your hand on the baby's arm. Tell the baby: "This is your arm."
3. Put your hand on the baby's tummy. Tell the baby: "This is your tummy."
4. Put your hands on the baby's ears. Tell the baby: "These are your ears."
5. Put your finger on the baby's nose. Tell the baby: "This is your nose."
6. Put your hands on the baby's knees. Tell the baby: "These are your knees."
7. Put your hand on the baby's foot. Tell the baby: "This is your foot."
8. Do all the things again in 1, 2, 3, 4, 5, 6, and 7.
9. If the baby makes a sound that is like a word you said, tell the baby how good he or she is. Smile and say the word again. You can do this over and over again.

❏ *Approval* ❏ *Trust*
● **YOU AND THE BABY SPEND SOME SPECIAL TIME WHEN YOU ARE THINKING ONLY ABOUT THE BABY (3-5 minutes).**
1. Go to a quiet place.

2. You will want to hold the baby close to you so that he or she can see your eyes and you can see the baby's face.
3. Be sure that you and the baby can see each other's eyes.
4. Talk to the baby. Have your voice be soft and gentle. The way you talk should let the baby know that you like him or her and like to be with him or her.
5. When the baby makes a noise, make the same noise back to the baby. If the baby makes a face, do the same thing back to the baby.
6. The baby learns by looking at your face and by hearing your voice. When you are talking to the baby, have your voice and face change. Show him or her that you are happy, surprised, or loving.

❏ *Trust*
● **THE WAY TO GIVE THE BABY A BATH.**
1. Get all the things you will need for the bath: towel, washcloth, soap, bath toy, powder, or anything else you will need. Put them where the baby will have the bath. You can use a tub made for a baby's bath or maybe use the sink in the kitchen.
2. Make water as deep as your finger is long. Feel the water with your hand or elbow. Be sure that it's not too hot or too cold.
3. Put the baby down on the bed, floor, or table and take off all the clothes.
4. Talk to the baby. The baby will hear the sound of your voice and will learn from it.
5. Put the baby in the water on his or her back. Be sure to hold the head out of the water. Tell the baby how nice it is to have a bath. The baby will learn that a bath is a good thing by hearing the NICE WAY you are talking.
6. Be sure to hold the back of the baby's head all the time. Put soap on a soft washcloth. Wash the baby; being sure that you don't rub too hard. Wash baby all over…also hair.
7. When baby makes a noise, you make a noise back to the baby. If the baby moves his or her arms or legs to splash the water, you can play along with the baby. Make a bath a FUN time.
8. Take the baby out of the water, holding gently. Lay the baby on the towel and dry gently. Put on any powders or creams that you use on the baby.
9. Put a diaper on the baby. Dress the baby. Keep talking to baby and look into baby's eyes.
10. Pick up baby and give a BIG HUG!

❏ *Approval* ❏ *Trust* ❏ *Acceptance*

● **HELP THE BABY MOVE AND PLAY.**

1. Put a blanket (or something soft) on the floor.
2. Put the baby on the blanket that is on the floor. The baby should be on his or her back.
3. Be sure that you and the baby can see each other's eyes.
4. Smile and keep talking to the baby when you are doing these things.
5. The baby is on his or her back on the floor. You will want to hold the baby by the shoulders. (Put each of your hands under each shoulder with your thumb on the front part of the baby's shoulder. Your fingers will be going up on the baby's back and helping to hold the baby's head.) You should be gentle when your hands are on the baby. Gently bring the baby up a little bit so that he or she is half way to sitting up. Now gently move the baby back to being on his or her back on the floor. (Do this five times.)
6. The baby will be on the floor on his or her back. Gently put each of your hands under the baby's knees. Slowly and gently move the baby's legs so that the knees are bent near the baby's tummy. Then slowly and gently move the legs back down on the floor (Do this five times.)

❏ *Approval* ❏ *Responsibility*
❏ *Respect for Others* ❏ *Flexibility*

● **HOW TO GET THE BABY AWAY FROM SOMETHING THAT IS NOT "OKAY" TO DOING SOMETHING THAT IS "OKAY."**

1. You see the baby doing something that he or she should not be doing. Pick up the baby and move to a place where he or she can do something that you think is "OK". You may have to gently hold the baby's hands and move the hands to some thing that is "OK" to do.
2. When you have the baby change what he or she is doing, have your voice and face show the baby that you are nice and kind instead of being angry.
3. If the baby pulls on a lamp cord, pick the baby up. Move the baby to a place where he or she can do something that is "OK." You may want to give him or her a toy to play with or put him or her someplace where playthings are near.

4. When the baby plays with a toy or talks to it, tell the baby that you like the way he or she is playing and that he or she is playing in a good place. (Example: "You are sitting by the table. I like that.")
5. When the baby changes from doing something bad to doing something good, tell the baby how good he or she is. Then, give a warm, loving touch or hug.

❏ *Trust*

● **SPEND SOME TIME WITH THE BABY WHEN THE THINGS YOU DO ARE MORE QUIET.**

1. Hold the baby in your arms. When you do this, have the head at your elbow. The baby's body will rest on the front of your arm and your hand will hold him or her at the bottom or rear. The baby will rest on your waist.
2. Look into each other's eyes.
3. Smile at the baby.
4. Talk softly and gently to the baby.
5. Walk around the room holding the baby. Tell the baby about the things in the room. This is the way a baby learns about things. Say, "This is a table and we can sit here in the chair and do things on the table." Do this with the other things in the room.
6. Hold the baby in front of a mirror so that the baby can see himself or herself.
7. When the baby makes a sound, smile at the baby or give him or her a hug. The baby will learn that this is good to do.

❏ *Trust* ❏ *Flexibility*

● **THE RIGHT WAY TO GIVE OR HAND A BABY FROM YOU TO SOMEONE ELSE.**

1. This is something to do SLOWLY and CAREFULLY.
2. Hold the back part of the baby's head with one hand. Use your other hand to hold the baby's rear or bottom.
3. Stand close to the other person when you are ready to hand over the baby.
4. Hand the baby to the other person.
5. When you give the baby to the other person, smile and say the baby's name…using a nice soft voice.

❏ *Approval* ❏ *Trust*

● **THE WAY TO FEED THE BABY WITH A BOTTLE.**
1. Go to a quiet place to feed the baby.
2. Hold bottle in the hand you use for writing. Hold baby in other arm…head resting at your elbow…body resting on the front part of your arm…your hand holding the baby's bottom…the baby resting on your waist.
3. Talk softly to the baby but do not use baby talk. The baby will then hear the right way to talk. Talk to the baby about something and SMILE!
4. SMILE and look into baby's eyes.
5. Sing songs to the baby like "Mary Had a Little Lamb" or "London Bridge"…or any song you like…the baby will like the sound.
6. Baby may want to hold the bottle himself or herself. This is okay!
7. Burp the baby.

❏ *Approval* ❏ *Trust* ❏ *Sense of Power*

● **HERE ARE THINGS TO SAY TO THE BABY WHILE YOU PUT THE DIAPER ON. (Talk to the baby but do not ask questions. Talk softly, look happy, and use your hands gently when doing these things.)**
1. Hold the baby's hand. Tell the baby: "This is your hand."
2. Put your hand on the baby's arm. Tell the baby: "This is your arm."
3. Put your hand on the baby's tummy. Tell the baby: "This is your tummy."
4. Put your hands on the baby's ears. Tell the baby: "These are your ears."
5. Put your finger on the baby's nose. Tell the baby: "This is your nose."
6. Put your hands on the baby's knees. Tell the baby: "These are your knees."
7. Put your hand on the baby's foot. Tell the baby: "This is your foot."
8. Do all the things again in 1, 2, 3, 4, 5, 6, and 7.
9. If the baby makes a sound that is like a word you said, tell the baby how good he or she is. Smile and say the word again. You can do this over and over again.

❏ *Approval* ❏ *Trust*

● **YOU AND THE BABY SPEND SOME SPECIAL TIME WHEN YOU ARE THINKING ONLY ABOUT THE BABY (3-5 minutes).**
1. Go to a quiet place.
2. You will want to hold the baby close to you so that he or she can see your eyes and you

can see the baby's face.
3. Be sure that you and the baby can see each other's eyes.
4. Talk to the baby. Have your voice be soft and gentle. The way you talk should let the baby know that you like him or her and like to be with him or her.
5. When the baby makes a noise, make the same noise back to the baby. If the baby makes a face, do the same thing back to the baby.
6. The baby learns by looking at your face and by hearing your voice. When you are talking to the baby, have your voice and face change. Show him or her that you are happy, surprised, or loving.

❏ *Trust*

● **THE WAY TO GIVE THE BABY A BATH.**
1. Get all the things you will need for the bath: towel, washcloth, soap, bath toy, powder, or anything else you will need. Put them where the baby will have the bath. You can use a tub made for a baby's bath or maybe use the sink in the kitchen.
2. Make water as deep as your finger is long. Feel the water with your hand or elbow. Be sure that it's not too hot or too cold.
3. Put the baby down on the bed, floor, or table and take off all the clothes.
4. Talk to the baby. The baby will hear the sound of your voice and will learn from it.
5. Put the baby in the water on his or her back. Be sure to hold the head out of the water. Tell the baby how nice it is to have a bath. The baby will learn that a bath is a good thing by hearing the NICE WAY you are talking.
6. Be sure to hold the back of the baby's head all the time. Put soap on a soft washcloth. Wash the baby; being sure that you don't rub too hard. Wash baby all over…also hair.
7. When baby makes a noise, you make a noise back to the baby. If the baby moves his or her arms or legs to splash the water, you can play along with the baby. Make a bath a FUN time.
8. Take the baby out of the water, holding gently. Lay the baby on the towel and dry gently. Put on any powders or creams that you use on the baby.
9. Put a diaper on the baby. Dress the baby. Keep talking to baby and look into baby's eyes.
10. Pick up baby and give a BIG HUG!

❏ *Approval* ❏ *Trust* ❏ *Acceptance*

● **HELP THE BABY MOVE AND PLAY.**
1. Put a blanket (or something soft) on the floor.
(continued…)

2. Put the baby on the blanket that is on the floor. The baby should be on his or her back.

3. Be sure that you and the baby can see each other's eyes.

4. Smile and keep talking to the baby when you are doing these things.

5. The baby is on his or her back on the floor. You will want to hold the baby by the shoulders. (Put each of your hands under each shoulder with your thumb on the front part of the baby's shoulder. Your fingers will be going up on the baby's back and helping to hold the baby's head.) You should be gentle when your hands are on the baby. Gently bring the baby up a little bit so that he or she is half way to sitting up. Now gently move the baby back to being on his or her back on the floor. (Do this five times.)

6. The baby will be on the floor on his or her back. Gently put each of your hands under the baby's knees. Slowly and gently move the baby's legs so that the knees are bent near the baby's tummy. Then slowly and gently move the legs back down on the floor (Do this five times.)

❒ *Approval* ❒ *Responsibility*
❒ *Respect for Others* ❒ *Flexibility*

● **HOW TO GET THE BABY AWAY FROM SOMETHING THAT IS NOT "OKAY" TO DOING SOMETHING THAT IS "OKAY."**

1. You see the baby doing something that he or she should not be doing. Pick up the baby and move to a place where he or she can do something that you think is "OK". You may have to gently hold the baby's hands and move the hands to some thing that is "OK" to do.

2. When you have the baby change what he or she is doing, have your voice and face show the baby that you are nice and kind instead of being angry.

3. If the baby pulls on a lamp cord, pick the baby up. Move the baby to a place where he or she can do something that is "OK." You may want to give him or her a toy to play with or put him or her someplace where playthings are near.

4. When the baby plays with a toy or talks to it, tell the baby that you like the way he or she is playing and that he or she is playing in a good place. (Example: "You are sitting by the table. I like that.")

5. When the baby changes from doing something bad to doing something good, tell the baby how good he or she is. Then, give a warm, loving touch or hug.

❒ *Trust*

● **SPEND SOME TIME WITH THE BABY WHEN THE THINGS YOU DO ARE MORE QUIET.**

1. Hold the baby in your arms. When you do this, have the head at your elbow. The baby's body will rest on the front of your arm and your hand will hold him or her at the bottom or rear. The baby will rest on your waist.

2. Look into each other's eyes.

3. Smile at the baby.

4. Talk softly and gently to the baby.

5. Walk around the room holding the baby. Tell the baby about the things in the room. This is the way a baby learns about things. Say, "This is a table and we can sit here in the chair and do things on the table." Do this with the other things in the room.

6. Hold the baby in front of a mirror so that the baby can see himself or herself.

7. When the baby makes a sound, smile at the baby or give him or her a hug. The baby will learn that this is good to do.

❒ *Approval* ❒ *Sense of Power*

● **PLAYING WITH THE BABY.**

1. Put the baby on your lap on his or her back (head at your knees).

2. Be sure that you and baby can see each other's eyes.

3. Smile at the baby.

4. Play the game "Peek-A-Boo" with the baby. Gently hold the baby's hands. Move the two hands so that they will be over the baby's eyes. When you are doing this you say "Peek-A". Now, take the hands off the eyes and say "Boo". This game shows the baby that you can go away *and* come back. Smile at the baby. Some of the time you may want to move your hands on and off your eyes while you say "Peek-A-Boo".

❒ *Trust* ❒ *Flexibility*

● **THE RIGHT WAY TO GIVE OR HAND A BABY FROM YOU TO SOMEONE ELSE.**

1. This is something to do SLOWLY and CAREFULLY.

2. Hold the back part of the baby's head with one hand. Use your other hand to hold the baby's rear or bottom.

3. Stand close to the other person when you are ready to hand over the baby.

4. Hand the baby to the other person.

5. When you give the baby to the other person, smile and say the baby's name...using a nice soft voice.

❑ *Approval* ❑ *Sense of Power*

● **PLAYING WITH THE BABY.**

1. Put the baby on your lap on his or her back (head at your knees).
2. Be sure that you and baby can see each other's eyes.
3. Smile at the baby.
4. Play the game "Peek-A-Boo" with the baby. Gently hold the baby's hands. Move the two hands so that they will be over the baby's eyes. When you are doing this you say "Peek-A". Now, take the hands off the eyes and say "Boo". This game shows the baby that you can go away *and* come back. Smile at the baby. Some of the time you may want to move your hands on and off your eyes while you say "Peek-A-Boo".

❑ *Approval* ❑ *Trust*

● **YOU AND THE BABY SPEND SOME SPECIAL TIME WHEN YOU ARE THINKING ONLY ABOUT THE BABY (3-5 minutes).**

1. Go to a quiet place.
2. You will want to hold the baby close to you so that he or she can see your eyes and you can see the baby's face.
3. Be sure that you and the baby can see each other's eyes.
4. Talk to the baby. Have your voice be soft and gentle. The way you talk should let the baby know that you like him or her and like to be with him or her.
5. When the baby makes a noise, make the same noise back to the baby. If the baby makes a face, do the same thing back to the baby.
6. The baby learns by looking at your face and by hearing your voice. When you are talking to the baby, have your voice and face change. Show him or her that you are happy, surprised, or loving.

❑ *Trust* ❑ *Flexibility*

● **THE RIGHT WAY TO GIVE OR HAND A BABY FROM YOU TO SOMEONE ELSE.**

1. This is something to do SLOWLY and CAREFULLY.
2. Hold the back part of the baby's head with one hand. Use your other hand to hold the baby's rear or bottom.
3. Stand close to the other person when you are ready to hand over the baby.
4. Hand the baby to the other person.
5. When you give the baby to the other person, smile and say the baby's name…using a nice soft voice.

❏ *Trust*

● **SPEND SOME TIME WITH THE BABY WHEN THE THINGS YOU DO ARE MORE QUIET.**

1. Hold the baby in your arms. When you do this, have the head at your elbow. The baby's body will rest on the front of your arm and your hand will hold him or her at the bottom or rear. The baby will rest on your waist.
2. Look into each other's eyes.
3. Smile at the baby.
4. Talk softly and gently to the baby.
5. Walk around the room holding the baby. Tell the baby about the things in the room. This is the way a baby learns about things. Show the baby a chair. Say, "This is a table and we can sit here in the chair and do things on the table." Show the baby a picture and say, "This is a picture of you when you were smaller." Do this with the other things in the room.
6. Hold the baby in front of a mirror so that the baby can see himself or herself.
7. When the baby makes a sound, smile at the baby or give him or her a hug. The baby will learn that this is good to do.

❏ *Approval* ❏ *Sense of Power*

● **PLAYING WITH THE BABY.**

1. Put the baby on your lap on his or her back (head at your knees).
2. Be sure that you and baby can see each other's eyes.
3. Smile at the baby.
4. Play the game "Peek-A-Boo" with the baby. Gently hold the baby's hands. Move the two hands so that they will be over the baby's eyes. When you are doing this you say "Peek-A". Now, take the hands off the eyes and say "Boo". This game shows the baby that you can go away *and* come back. Smile at the baby. Some of the time you may want to move your hands on and off your eyes while you say "Peek-A-Boo".

❏ *Approval* ❏ *Trust*

● **YOU AND THE BABY SPEND SOME SPECIAL TIME WHEN YOU ARE THINKING ONLY ABOUT THE BABY (3-5 minutes).**

1. Go to a quiet place.
2. You will want to hold the baby close to you so that he or she can see your eyes and you can see the baby's face.
3. Be sure that you and the baby can see each other's eyes.
4. Talk to the baby. Have your voice be soft and gentle. The way you talk should let the baby know that you like him or her and like to be with him or her.
5. When the baby makes a noise, make the same noise back to the baby. If the baby makes a face, do the same thing back to the baby.
6. The baby learns by looking at your face and by hearing your voice. When you are talking to the baby, have your voice and face change. Show him or her that you are happy, surprised, or loving.

❏ *Trust* ❏ *Flexibility*

● **THE RIGHT WAY TO GIVE OR HAND A BABY FROM YOU TO SOMEONE ELSE.**

1. This is something to do SLOWLY and CAREFULLY.
2. Hold the back part of the baby's head with one hand. Use your other hand to hold the baby's rear or bottom.
3. Stand close to the other person when you are ready to hand over the baby.
4. Hand the baby to the other person.
5. When you give the baby to the other person, smile and say the baby's name...using a nice soft voice.

Level 3 Characteristics

- Stands alone
- Understands one step command (but may not follow it)
- Points to things desired
- Toddles
- Crawls upstairs
- Says 5 to 6 words (spoken language)
- 50+ words understood
- Says thank you
- Looks at details on toys
- Claps hands
- Learning to drink from a cup
- Holds cup with two hands

Level 3 Information

Self-esteem is a feeling.
If you have HIGH self-esteem...

> You make good friends!
> You care about yourself and other people;
> You are responsible;
> You enjoy learning;
> You are proud of what you do;
> You can handle failure;
> You can share feelings.

HIGH self-esteem is having a GOOD feeling about yourself, your place in the family, your school, and your world.

THINGS TO REMEMBER:

- When the child does something good or right...tell him or her so.
- Use a NICE voice.
- Use the child's name when you talk to him or her.
- If the child does not do something right... it is okay and the child is okay.
- Do not use foul language in front of the child.
- When the child shares...tell him or her that it's a GOOD thing to do.
- FIND A REASON TO SAY EACH OF THESE PHRASES AT LEAST ONCE A DAY:
  Wonderful!
  I like what you are doing.
  I like to see you smile.

DON'T GIVE UP!

— If the child does not want to do the activity with you the way you want him or her to...try again tomorrow.

— Keep trying. This is the way you **SHOW** the child that you mean what you say. A child needs to **TRUST** in order to share with you or listen to you.

— **HOW** you say something is sometimes more important than **WHAT** you say.

You may be doing MOST of these things already as part of the way you care for children and run your home. By doing these things in the way they are written, you will be helping the child's self-esteem **plus** your own self-esteem.

When you can help somebody feel good... you feel good!

The BASE program is about helping children have HIGH self-esteem. It is a group of things to do and share with a child. These things are short, simple and positive. They should be done everyday when possible.

REMEMBER:

If any of these things do not agree with the way you believe or your religion (example: dancing), do not do it.

❏ *Approval* ❏ *Trust* ❏ *Sense of Power*
● **AT THE SAME TIME EACH DAY, YOU AND THE CHILD SPEND SOME SPECIAL TIME TOGETHER.**
1. Slowly walk around the living room holding the child in your arms.
2. Talk to the child. Have your voice be soft and gentle. The look on your face and your voice should change to go with what you are saying. Your face and words might show that you are happy, surprised or loving.
3. As you walk around, say the names of the things you see in the room (dog, chair, picture, book).
4. If the child looks at something, say the name of the thing to the child (say, "Rug"—then point to the rug).
5. Go to a mirror. Hold the child in front of the mirror. Say the child's name as he or she looks at himself or herself. ("Look at Mike in the mirror!")

❏ *Acceptance* ❏ *Responsibility* ❏ *Flexibility*
● **HOW TO GET THE CHILD AWAY FROM SOMETHING THAT IS NOT "OKAY" TO DOING SOMETHING THAT IS "OKAY".**
• The child should learn to stay away from a place that may be DANGEROUS (like under the sink, by the stove, near light plugs).
• The child should learn to stay away from a place that you think is an OFF-LIMITS spot.
• The child should learn not to pull on things like a tablecloth, drapes, a dog's ear, lamp cord, or any other thing that you feel it is not right to do.
• You can say NO to the child. This should be done so the child knows that you mean what you say. Then:
  1. Move him or her away from the activity he or she should not be doing.
  2. Be gentle and show the child you are not mad at him or her while doing this.
  3. Move the child to a place where he or she can play with a toy, or do something that is okay and safe.
  4. Stay with the child long enough to be sure that he or she will begin to play with the toy you gave him or her.
  5. Tell the child that you like what he or she is doing now. (You want to have the child learn what is right and what is wrong to do. **It's up to you to show the child.**)

❏ *Approval* ❏ *Respect for Others*
● **WHILE YOU SPEND TIME PLAYING WITH THE CHILD, TEACH HIM TO DO SOME THINGS. The child should begin to learn to do what you say. (You will need three or four small soft things like cotton balls, or soft blocks, or marshmallows. Then you need a pot, basket, or something with a big opening at the top. The small things have to fit into the pot or basket.)**
1. Have the child sit on the floor. Put pot in front of child.
2. Take one of the "small" things and drop it into the pot. Say: "I put in!" (Do it three more times).
3. Put one of the small things into the child's hand.
4. Look into the child's eyes and say: "Now— you put in!" If he cannot do it on his or her own, give help.
5. If the child does it, say: "Great!" or "I like that!"
6. SMILE and HUG!
7. Keep playing for a short time. Stop before the child gets tired or begins to cry.

❏ *Approval* ❏ *Acceptance*
● **HELP THE CHILD LEARN TO FEEL GOOD AND HAPPY.**
1. Look at the child during the day. When you see the child is happy—think about what is making the child feel this way and say something about it. ("You look so *happy!*", "I like your smile!", "You are making such funny noises!", "You have such a great laugh!") You want the child to learn the things that make him or her feel good.
2. The child should learn that mealtime is a time to feel good.
3. Use a warm, gentle voice when you talk to the child.
4. Smile at the child and talk to him or her using a "happy" voice.

❏ *Approval* ❏ *Trust* ❏ *Sense of Power*
● **IF THE CHILD IS NOT WALKING ALONE, HERE ARE SOME THINGS YOU CAN DO WITH THE CHILD.**
1. The child should be standing.
2. Stand in front of the child. Bend so that you can look into the child's eyes and so the child can see your face without having to look up too far.
3. Have the child hold on to your fingers (the fingers next to your thumbs).

(continued...)

4. The child's arms should be out towards you. Bend down so the child's arms go straight out and not up towards your face. (If this does not help the child, put your hands under the child's arms.)

5. Take a few steps backwards and try to get the child to follow you by moving his or her feet forward, towards you. (GO SLOWLY.)

6. If the child stands still and does not move his or her feet—just say something nice to the child. ("You are standing so tall!" or "Look how big you are!")

7. If the child does begin to walk—keep walking backwards. Tell the child how PROUD you are—use the child's name. ("You are taking such big steps!")

8. After you have walked awhile, gently help the child to sit down on the floor.

9. Give a HUG! Smile so that he or she knows that he or she has done something good.

❏ *Approval* ❏ *Trust* ❏ *Sense of Power*

● **AT THE SAME TIME EACH DAY, YOU AND THE CHILD SPEND SOME SPECIAL TIME TOGETHER.**
1. Slowly walk around the living room holding the child in your arms.
2. Talk to the child. Have your voice be soft and gentle. The look on your face and your voice should change to go with what you are saying. Your face and words might show that you are happy, surprised or loving.
3. As you walk around, say the names of the things you see in the room (dog, chair, picture, book).
4. If the child looks at something, say the name of the thing to the child (say, "Rug"—then point to the rug).
5. Go to a mirror. Hold the child in front of the mirror. Say the child's name as he or she looks at himself or herself. ("Look at Mike in the mirror!")

❏ *Acceptance* ❏ *Responsibility* ❏ *Flexibility*

● **HOW TO GET THE CHILD AWAY FROM SOMETHING THAT IS NOT "OKAY" TO DOING SOMETHING THAT IS "OKAY".**
• The child should learn to stay away from a place that may be DANGEROUS (like under the sink, by the stove, near light plugs).
• The child should learn to stay away from a place that you think is an OFF-LIMITS spot.
• The child should learn not to pull on things like a tablecloth, drapes, a dog's ear, lamp cord, or any other thing that you feel it is not right to do.
• You can say NO to the child. This should be done so the child knows that you mean what you say. Then:
  1. Move him or her away from the activity he or she should not be doing.
  2. Be gentle and show the child you are not mad at him or her while doing this.
  3. Move the child to a place where he or she can play with a toy, or do something that is okay and safe.
  4. Stay with the child long enough to be sure that he or she will begin to play with the toy you gave him or her.
  5. Tell the child that you like what he or she is doing now. (You want to have the child learn what is right and what is wrong to do. **It's up to you to show the child.)**

❏ *Approval* ❏ *Respect for Others*

● **WHILE YOU SPEND TIME PLAYING WITH THE CHILD, TEACH HIM TO DO SOME THINGS. The child should begin to learn to do what you say. (You will need three or four small soft things like cotton balls, or soft blocks, or marshmallows. Then you need a pot, basket, or something with a big opening at the top. The small things have to fit into the pot or basket.)**
1. Have the child sit on the floor. Put pot in front of child.
2. Take one of the "small" things and drop it into the pot. Say: "I put in!" (Do it three more times).
3. Put one of the small things into the child's hand.
4. Look into the child's eyes and say: "Now— you put in!" If he cannot do it on his or her own, give help.
5. If the child does it, say: "Great!" or "I like that!"
6. SMILE and HUG!
7. Keep playing for a short time. Stop before the child gets tired or begins to cry.

❏ *Approval* ❏ *Acceptance*

● **HELP THE CHILD LEARN TO FEEL GOOD AND HAPPY.**
1. Look at the child during the day. When you see the child is happy—think about what is making the child feel this way and say something about it. ("You look so *happy!*", "I like your smile!", "You are making such funny noises!", "You have such a great laugh!") You want the child to learn the things that make him or her feel good.
2. The child should learn that mealtime is a time to feel good.
3. Use a warm, gentle voice when you talk to the child.
4. Smile at the child and talk to him or her using a "happy" voice.

❏ *Approval* ❏ *Trust* ❏ *Sense of Power*

● **IF THE CHILD IS NOT WALKING ALONE, HERE ARE SOME THINGS YOU CAN DO WITH THE CHILD.**
1. The child should be standing.
2. Stand in front of the child. Bend so that you can look into the child's eyes and so the child can see your face without having to look up too far.
3. Have the child hold on to your fingers (the fingers next to your thumbs).

(continued...)

4. The child's arms should be out towards you. Bend down so the child's arms go straight out and not up towards your face. (If this does not help the child, put your hands under the child's arms.)

5. Take a few steps backwards and try to get the child to follow you by moving his or her feet forward, towards you. (GO SLOWLY.)

6. If the child stands still and does not move his or her feet—just say something nice to the child. ("You are standing so tall!" or "Look how big you are!")

7. If the child does begin to walk—keep walking backwards. Tell the child how PROUD you are—use the child's name. ("You are taking such big steps!")

8. After you have walked awhile, gently help the child to sit down on the floor.

9. Give a HUG! Smile so that he or she knows that he or she has done something good.

❏ *Approval* ❏ *Trust* ❏ *Sense of Power*
● **TEACH THE CHILD TO TOUCH SOMETHING IN A NICE WAY.**
1. Put the child on your lap.
2. Gently touch or rub the child's hand. Say: "This is GENTLE!"
3. Hold the child's hand and have him or her gently touch or rub your other hand. Say: "Now you are being gentle."
4. Stroke the child's hair gently with your hand and say, "This is GENTLE!"
5. Show him or her how to stroke your hair gently.
6. Repeat two or three times.
7. End with a Big HUG!

❏ *Approval* ❏ *Sense of Power*
● **SPEND SOME TIME PLAYING WITH THE CHILD.**
1. You and the child should sit on the floor, across from each other, so that both of you will see each other's face.
2. Be sure that you and the child can see each other's eyes.
3. Smile at the child.
4. Clap your hands. Now you will show the child how to clap his or her hands. Your two hands will hold each of the child's two hands. Bring the hands together to make a "CLAP".
5. Laugh with the child.
6. When the child knows how to clap hands, the two of you can play a game, "Pat-A-Cake".
7. As you say each line, do what the song says to do—still holding the child's hands (clap your hands where there is a • above the word).

• • • • • • • • • • •

Pat-a-Cake. Pat-a-Cake. Baker's Man. Bake a

• • • • • •

Cake as Fast as You Can.
Roll it, and Roll it, and Put it in a Pan.

• • • • • • • • •

Pat-a-Cake. Pat-a-Cake. Baker's Man.
8. Hug child.

❏ *Approval* ❏ *Trust* ❏ *Sense of Power*

● **TEACH THE CHILD TO TOUCH SOMETHING IN A NICE WAY.**

1. Put the child on your lap.
2. Gently touch or rub the child's hand. Say: "This is GENTLE!"
3. Hold the child's hand and have him or her gently touch or rub your other hand. Say: "Now you are being gentle."
4. Stroke the child's hair gently with your hand and say, "This is GENTLE!"
5. Show him or her how to stroke your hair gently.
6. Repeat two or three times.
7. End with a Big HUG!

❏ *Approval* ❏ *Sense of Power*

● **SPEND SOME TIME PLAYING WITH THE CHILD.**

1. You and the child should sit on the floor, across from each other, so that both of you will see each other's face.
2. Be sure that you and the child can see each other's eyes.
3. Smile at the child.
4. Clap your hands. Now you will show the child how to clap his or her hands. Your two hands will hold each of the child's two hands. Bring the hands together to make a "CLAP".
5. Laugh with the child.
6. When the child knows how to clap hands, the two of you can play a game, "Pat-A-Cake".
7. As you say each line, do what the song says to do—still holding the child's hands (clap your hands where there is a • above the word).

   • • •   • • •   • •   • •   •

Pat-a-Cake. Pat-a-Cake. Baker's Man. Bake a

   • • • • • •

Cake as Fast as You Can.
Roll it, and Roll it, and Put it in a Pan.

   • • • • • • • • •

Pat-a-Cake. Pat-a-Cake. Baker's Man.
8. Hug child.

❏ *Approval* ❏ *Acceptance*

● **HELP THE CHILD LEARN TO FEEL GOOD AND HAPPY.**

1. Look at the child during the day. When you see the child is happy—think about what is making the child feel this way and say something about it. ("You look so *happy!*", "I like your smile!", "You are making such funny noises!", "You have such a great laugh!") You want the child to learn the things that make him or her feel good.
2. The child should learn that mealtime is a time to feel good.
3. Use a warm, gentle voice when you talk to the child.
4. Smile at the child and talk to him or her using a "happy" voice.

❏ *Approval* ❏ *Trust* ❏ *Sense of Power*

● **IF THE CHILD IS NOT WALKING ALONE, HERE ARE SOME THINGS YOU CAN DO WITH THE CHILD.**

1. The child should be standing.
2. Stand in front of the child. Bend so that you can look into the child's eyes and so the child can see your face without having to look up too far.
3. Have the child hold on to your fingers (the fingers next to your thumbs).
4. The child's arms should be out towards you. Bend down so the child's arms go straight out and not up towards your face. (If this does not help the child, put your hands under the child's arms.)
5. Take a few steps backwards and try to get the child to follow you by moving his or her feet forward, towards you. (GO SLOWLY.)
6. If the child stands still and does not move his or her feet—just say something nice to the child. ("You are standing so tall!" or "Look how big you are!")
7. If the child does begin to walk—keep walking backwards. Tell the child how PROUD you are—use the child's name. ("You are taking such big steps!")
8. After you have walked awhile, gently help the child to sit down on the floor.
9. Give a HUG! Smile so that he or she knows that he or she has done something good.

❏ *Acceptance* ❏ *Responsibility* ❏ *Flexibility*

● **HOW TO GET THE CHILD AWAY FROM SOMETHING THAT IS NOT "OKAY" TO DOING SOMETHING THAT IS "OKAY".**

• The child should learn to stay away from a place that may be DANGEROUS (like under the sink, by the stove, near light plugs).
• The child should learn to stay away from a place that you think is an OFF-LIMITS spot.
• The child should learn not to pull on things like a tablecloth, drapes, a dog's ear, lamp cord, or any other thing that you feel it is not right to do.
• You can say NO to the child. This should be done so the child knows that you mean what you say. Then:

1. Move him or her away from the activity he or she should not be doing.
2. Be gentle and show the child you are not mad at him or her while doing this.
3. Move the child to a place where he or she can play with a toy, or do something that is okay and safe.
4. Stay with the child long enough to be sure that he or she will begin to play with the toy you gave him or her.
5. Tell the child that you like what he or she is doing now. (You want to have the child learn what is right and what is wrong to do. It's up to you to show the child.)

❏ *Approval* ❏ *Acceptance*

● **HELP THE CHILD LEARN TO FEEL GOOD AND HAPPY.**

1. Look at the child during the day. When you see the child is happy think about what is making the child feel this way and say something about it. ("You look so *happy!*", "I like your smile!", "You are making such funny noises!", "You have such a great laugh!") You want the child to learn the things that make him or her feel good.
2. The child should learn that mealtime is a time to feel good.
3. Use a warm, gentle voice when you talk to the child.
4. Smile at the child and talk to him or her using a "happy" voice.

❏ *Approval* ❏ *Trust* ❏ *Sense of Power*

● **IF THE CHILD IS NOT WALKING ALONE, HERE ARE SOME THINGS YOU CAN DO WITH THE CHILD.**

1. The child should be standing.
2. Stand in front of the child. Bend so that you can look into the child's eyes and so the child can see your face without having to look up too far.
3. Have the child hold on to your fingers (the fingers next to your thumbs).
4. The child's arms should be out towards you. Bend down so the child's arms go straight out and not up towards your face. (If this does not help the child, put your hands under the child's arms.)
5. Take a few steps backwards and try to get the child to follow you by moving his or her feet forward, towards you. (GO SLOWLY.)
6. If the child stands still and does not move his or her feet—just say something nice to the child. ("You are standing so tall!" or "Look how big you are!")
7. If the child does begin to walk—keep walking backwards. Tell the child how PROUD you are—use the child's name. ("You are taking such big steps!")
8. After you have walked awhile, gently help the child to sit down on the floor.
9. Give a HUG! Smile so that he or she knows that he or she has done something good.

❏ *Approval* ❏ *Sense of Power*

● **SPEND SOME TIME PLAYING WITH THE CHILD.**

1. You and the child should sit on the floor, across from each other, so that both of you will see each other's face.
2. Be sure that you and the child can see each other's eyes.
3. Smile at the child.
4. Clap your hands. Now you will show the child how to clap his or her hands. Your two hands will hold each of the child's two hands. Bring the hands together to make a "CLAP".
5. Laugh with the child.
6. When the child knows how to clap hands, the two of you can play a game, "Pat-A-Cake".
7. As you say each line, do what the song says to do—still holding the child's hands (clap your hands where there is a • above the word).

  • •   • • • •   • •   • •
Pat-a-Cake. Pat-a-Cake. Baker's Man. Bake a
  • •   • • •
Cake as Fast as You Can.
Roll it, and Roll it, and Put it in a Pan.
  • •   • • • •   •
Pat-a-Cake. Pat-a-Cake. Baker's Man.
8. Hug child.

15-24 months

Level 4 Characteristics

- Climbs
- Walks
- Turns pages, 2 to 3 at a time
- Scribbles
- Feeds self, spilling 50%
- Says approximately 12 words
- Understands over 100 words
- Follows simple directions
- Everything is "mine"
- Emergence of self (non-compliance)
- Cognitive development (imitation)
- Object permanency (ability to remember non-present objects or persons)

Level 4 Information

Self-esteem is a feeling.
If you have HIGH self-esteem...
> You make good friends!
> You care about yourself and other people;
> You are responsible;
> You enjoy learning;
> You are proud of what you do;
> You can handle failure;
> You can share feelings.

HIGH self-esteem is having a GOOD feeling about yourself, your place in the family, your school, and your world.

THINGS TO REMEMBER:
- It is VERY important that the child has something of his or her OWN.
- PRAISE whenever possible!
- Use the child's name when talking with him or her.
- Do not use foul language in front of the child.
- By spending special time with the child, you are telling him or her that you CARE. The child thinks: "If you care about me, then maybe I am worth caring about!"
- Keep adult sexual activity private.
- FIND A REASON TO SAY EACH OF THESE PHRASES AT LEAST ONCE A DAY:
  That's the way!
  I'm proud of you!

DON'T GIVE UP!
— If the child does not want to do the activity with you the way you want him or her to...try again tomorrow.
— Keep trying. This is the way you **SHOW** the child that you mean what you say. A child needs to **TRUST** in order to share with you or listen to you.
— **HOW** you say something is sometimes more important than **WHAT** you say.

You may be doing MOST of these things already as part of the way you care for children and run your home. By doing these things in the way they are written, you will be helping the child's self-esteem **plus** your own self-esteem.

When you can help somebody feel good... you feel good!

The BASE program is about helping children have HIGH self-esteem. It is a group of things to do and share with a child. These things are short, simple and positive. They should be done everyday when possible.

REMEMBER:
If any of these things do not agree with the way you believe or your religion (example: dancing), do not do it.

❑ *Approval* ❑ *Trust*
❑ *Acceptance* ❑ *Self-Respect*

● **A CHILD NEEDS TO KNOW THAT HE OR SHE IS DOING THE RIGHT THING. WHEN YOU SEE THAT HE OR SHE IS BEING GOOD, BE SURE TO TELL HIM OR HER WHY YOU LIKED WHAT HE OR SHE DID.**

1. Some good things may be the way he or she plays with a toy, comes to you when called, does what you ask.
2. Here are the kind of things you can tell the child:
   • That is such a pretty smile.
   • You made me so happy.
   • That is a big help to me.
   • You are so careful with your toys.
   • Kitty loves you. You are so gentle with Kitty.

❑ *Approval* ❑ *Trust*

● **A CHILD CAN LEARN THAT IT IS NICE TO BE TOUCHED AND TO TOUCH SOMEONE IN THE RIGHT WAY. THIS CAN BE DONE WHEN THE CHILD HAS A BATH.**

1. Give the child a bath when you do not have to hurry.
2. Never leave the child alone in the bath. This will help to keep the child safe.
3. The bath water should be warm, not hot or cold. Make the water as high as your hand. Do not let cool air into the bathroom. This would make the child cold.
4. Tell the child that you will help him or her take a bath.
5. Show the child how you rub soap on the washcloth.
6. Wash the child's body using the washcloth. While the child is being washed, tell the parts of the body. For example, "This is your foot." "I am washing your back."
7. If the child is good while having a bath, you should tell him or her that you like the way he or she acted. It is all right if the child makes some happy sounds and has fun making little splashes. You may want to hold one of the child's hands and show how to make little splashes.

❑ *Approval* ❑ *Trust* ❑ *Sense of Power*

● **GENTLY BRUSHING THE CHILD'S HAIR CAN HELP TEACH THE CHILD ANOTHER WAY TO TOUCH SOMEONE THE RIGHT WAY. THE CHILD WILL LEARN THAT THE GENTLE TOUCH FEELS GOOD.**

1. Brush the child's hair at a time when he or she feels good. This may be when he or she has just had food, the diapers or pants are dry, and he or she is not tired.
2. Use a comb or brush to fix the child's hair. Do this at a time when you do not have to rush. Pick a place that you both like.
3. Sit on the floor, and have the child between your two legs, so that you can reach the child's hair.
4. Tell him or her about pretty hair. "The hair is soft", and "You look so nice when your hair is brushed."
5. Tell him or her that he or she is sitting quietly, that he or she is being so good, that he or she is sitting close to you.
6. Start brushing the ends of the hair in short, soft strokes. Work out any tangles. Hold a bunch of hair near the head and brush out the tangles, brushing away from the head. Keep brushing closer to the head. Talk to him or her about being good and how nice it is to look good.
7. Let the child try to brush his or her hair. The child can also brush or comb a doll's hair.
8. Tell the child you like the way he or she is being gentle, helpful, careful, happy, acting so big, or anything else that is nice.
9. Give the child a hug and tell him or her that he or she looks nice.

❑ *Approval* ❑ *Trust* ❑ *Acceptance*

● **SPEND SOME TIME OUTSIDE WITH THE CHILD. THE CHILD NEEDS TO BE ABLE TO RUN AND PLAY OUTSIDE IN ORDER TO DEVELOP THE RIGHT WAY.**

1. Dress the right way for being outside. The child may need a jacket or snowshoes when it is cold, or shorts when it is hot.
2. Tell the child what the two of you are going to do outside (Example: go for a walk, look at the trees.)
3. When outside hold the child's hand and walk around slowly.

(continued...)

4. Name the things that you see as you walk, "See the bird," "There is a plane," "These leaves are green." If the child says the name of the things after you, tell him or her how good he or she is.
5. Go to a place where it is safe and let the child move and run around alone.
6. Tell the child things that will make him or her feel good, such as "You are so big," "You are such a good runner."
7. Stop playing outside when the child gets tired (or when you get tired).

❑ *Approval* ❑ *Trust* ❑ *Acceptance*

● **THE CHILD MAY LIKE TO HAVE HIS OR HER BACK RUBBED GENTLY WITH YOUR HAND. (DO NOT DO THIS IF THE CHILD THINKS YOU ARE TICKLING HIM OR HER OR DOES NOT LIKE IT.)**
1. Nap time, bed time, while watching TV, or any quiet time may be a good time to rub the child's back.
2. Tell the child how much you like him or her, how much you like to rub his or her back and be together.

❏ *Approval* ❏ *Trust*
❏ *Acceptance* ❏ *Self-Respect*

● **A CHILD NEEDS TO KNOW THAT HE OR SHE IS DOING THE RIGHT THING. WHEN YOU SEE THAT HE OR SHE IS BEING GOOD, BE SURE TO TELL HIM OR HER WHY YOU LIKED WHAT HE OR SHE DID.**

1. Some good things may be the way he or she plays with a toy, comes to you when called, does what you ask.
2. Here are the kind of things you can tell the child:
   • That is such a pretty smile.
   • You made me so happy.
   • That is a big help to me.
   • You are so careful with your toys.
   • Kitty loves you. You are so gentle with Kitty.

❏ *Approval* ❏ *Trust*

● **A CHILD CAN LEARN THAT IT IS NICE TO BE TOUCHED AND TO TOUCH SOMEONE IN THE RIGHT WAY. THIS CAN BE DONE WHEN THE CHILD HAS A BATH.**

1. Give the child a bath when you do not have to hurry.
2. Never leave the child alone in the bath. This will help to keep the child safe.
3. The bath water should be warm, not hot or cold. Make the water as high as your hand. Do not let cool air into the bathroom. This would make the child cold.
4. Tell the child that you will help him or her take a bath.
5. Show the child how you rub soap on the washcloth.
6. Wash the child's body using the washcloth. While the child is being washed, tell the parts of the body. For example, "This is your foot." "I am washing your back."
7. If the child is good while having a bath, you should tell him or her that you like the way he or she acted. It is all right if the child makes some happy sounds and has fun making little splashes. You may want to hold one of the child's hands and show how to make little splashes.

❏ *Approval* ❏ *Trust* ❏ *Acceptance*

● **SPEND SOME TIME OUTSIDE WITH THE CHILD. THE CHILD NEEDS TO BE ABLE TO RUN AND PLAY OUTSIDE IN ORDER TO DEVELOP THE RIGHT WAY.**

1. Dress the right way for being outside. The child may need a jacket or snowshoes when it is cold, or shorts when it is hot.
2. Tell the child what the two of you are going to do outside (Example: go for a walk, look at the trees.)
3. When outside hold the child's hand and walk around slowly.
4. Name the things that you see as you walk, "See the bird," "There is a plane," "These leaves are green." If the child says the name of the things after you, tell him or her how good he or she is.
5. Go to a place where it is safe and let the child move and run around alone.
6. Tell the child things that will make him or her feel good, such as "You are so big," "You are such a good runner."
7. Stop playing outside when the child gets tired (or when you get tired).

❏ *Approval* ❏ *Trust* ❏ *Respect for Others*

● **SPEND SOME TIME PLAYING WITH THE CHILD.**

1. Pick a time to play with the child when you will not have to hurry or have to do other things.
2. Pick three toys or things that the child could play with. You may pick a ball, a doll, pot and pans, cards, empty milk cartons, empty egg cartons, or anything else that you have.
3. Show the three things you picked to the child and let him or her pick one thing to play with.
4. Tell the child that he or she picked a good thing.
5. Play with the child and the object he or she picked. If it is a ball, you could roll it to each other. The child may choose some things that you could put one on top of the other in a stack, such as cards or boxes.
6. Play with the toy or object as long as the child is having fun.
7. Be sure to tell the child how much you like the way he or she is playing. You want the child to feel good about what he or she is doing.

❏ *Approval* ❏ *Acceptance*

● **A QUIET, HAPPY TIME IS WHEN YOU READ TO THE CHILD, OR TALK ABOUT PICTURES IN A BOOK OR MAGAZINE. THE CHILD MAY LIKE TO DO THIS FOR ONLY A VERY SHORT TIME.**

1. Have the child on your lap or next to you.
2. As you look at the pictures in the book or magazine, tell the child what you see and talk about it: "The cat is running.", "There is a door."
3. Point to things in bright colors and name them, like "pretty kitty." The child may try to say what you said.
4. If the child knows the name of some objects in a picture, point to them and let the child name them, such as a dog, chair, table.
5. Tell him or her how great it is that he or she can point to and say "DOG."

❏ *Approval* ❏ *Trust* ❏ *Acceptance*

● **THE CHILD MAY LIKE TO HAVE HIS OR HER BACK RUBBED GENTLY WITH YOUR HAND. (DO NOT DO THIS IF THE CHILD THINKS YOU ARE TICKLING HIM OR HER OR DOES NOT LIKE IT.)**

1. Nap time, bed time, while watching TV, or any quiet time may be a good time to rub the child's back.
2. Tell the child how much you like him or her, how much you like to rub his or her back and be together.

❏ *Approval* ❏ *Trust* ❏ *Respect for Others*

● **SPEND SOME TIME PLAYING WITH THE CHILD.**

1. Pick a time to play with the child when you will not have to hurry or have to do other things.
2. Pick three toys or things that the child could play with. You may pick a ball, a doll, pot and pans, cards, empty milk cartons, empty egg cartons, or anything else that you have.
3. Show the three things you picked to the child and let him or her pick one thing to play with.
4. Tell the child that he or she picked a good thing.
5. Play with the child and the object he or she picked. If it is a ball, you could roll it to each other. The child may choose some things that you could put one on top of the other in a stack, such as cards or boxes.
6. Play with the toy or object as long as the child is having fun.
7. Be sure to tell the child how much you like the way he or she is playing. You want the child to feel good about what he or she is doing.

❏ *Approval* ❏ *Trust*
❏ *Acceptance* ❏ *Self-Respect*

● **A CHILD NEEDS TO KNOW THAT HE OR SHE IS DOING THE RIGHT THING. WHEN YOU SEE THAT HE OR SHE IS BEING GOOD, BE SURE TO TELL HIM OR HER WHY YOU LIKED WHAT HE OR SHE DID.**

1. Some good things may be the way he or she plays with a toy, comes to you when called, does what you ask.
2. Here are the kind of things you can tell the child:
   • That is such a pretty smile.
   • You made me so happy.
   • That is a big help to me.
   • You are so careful with your toys.
   • Kitty loves you. You are so gentle with him or her.

❏ *Approval* ❏ *Acceptance*

● **A QUIET, HAPPY TIME IS WHEN YOU READ TO THE CHILD, OR TALK ABOUT PICTURES IN A BOOK OR MAGAZINE. THE CHILD MAY LIKE TO DO THIS FOR ONLY A VERY SHORT TIME.**

1. Have the child on your lap or next to you.
2. As you look at the pictures in the book or magazine, tell the child what you see and talk about it: "The cat is running.", "There is a door."
3. Point to things in bright colors and name them, like "pretty kitty." The child may try to say what you said.
4. If the child knows the name of some objects in a picture, point to them and let the child name them, such as a dog, chair, table.
5. Tell him or her how great it is that he or she can point to and say "DOG."

❏ Approval ❏ Trust ❏ Respect for Others

● **SPEND SOME TIME PLAYING WITH THE CHILD.**

1. Pick a time to play with the child when you will not have to hurry or have to do other things.
2. Pick three toys or things that the child could play with. You may pick a ball, a doll, pot and pans, cards, empty milk cartons, empty egg cartons, or anything else that you have.
3. Show the three things you picked to the child and let him or her pick one thing to play with.
4. Tell the child that he or she picked a good thing.
5. Play with the child and the object he or she picked. If it is a ball, you could roll it to each other. The child may choose some things that you could put one on top of the other in a stack, such as cards or boxes.
6. Play with the toy or object as long as the child is having fun.
7. Be sure to tell the child how much you like the way he or she is playing. You want the child to feel good about what he or she is doing.

❏ Approval ❏ Trust
❏ Acceptance ❏ Self-Respect

● **A CHILD NEEDS TO KNOW THAT HE OR SHE IS DOING THE RIGHT THING. WHEN YOU SEE THAT HE OR SHE IS BEING GOOD, BE SURE TO TELL HIM OR HER WHY YOU LIKED WHAT HE OR SHE DID.**

1. Some good things may be the way he or she plays with a toy, comes to you when called, does what you ask.
2. Here are the kind of things you can tell the child:
   • That is such a pretty smile.
   • You made me so happy.
   • That is a big help to me.
   • You are so careful with your toys.
   • Kitty loves you. You are so gentle with Kitty.

❏ Approval ❏ Acceptance

● **A QUIET, HAPPY TIME IS WHEN YOU READ TO THE CHILD, OR TALK ABOUT PICTURES IN A BOOK OR MAGAZINE. THE CHILD MAY LIKE TO DO THIS FOR ONLY A VERY SHORT TIME.**

1. Have the child on your lap or next to you.
2. As you look at the pictures in the book or magazine, tell the child what you see and talk about it: "The cat is running.", "There is a door."
3. Point to things in bright colors and name them, like "pretty kitty." The child may try to say what you said.
4. If the child knows the name of some objects in a picture, point to them and let the child name them, such as a dog, chair, table.
5. Tell him or her how great it is that he or she can point to and say "DOG."

❏ Approval ❏ Acceptance

● **YOU AND THE CHILD SPEND SOME SPECIAL TIME TOGETHER. PLAY THAT YOU ARE TALKING ON THE TELEPHONE.**

1. Find a quiet place for you to play together. You will need a toy telephone or pretend you are holding a phone to your ear.
2. Show the child how you say "Hello" on the phone.
3. Give the phone to the child and tell him or her to say "Hello" into the phone.
4. Play that you and the child are talking to each other on the phone. Use these words often: yes, no, hello, goodbye, and the child's name, "Hi, Johnny."
5. Let the child play that he or she is talking to a friend, Mickey Mouse or anyone else.
6. Tell the child that you liked the way he or she played.
7. If the child likes to do this, talk on the phone to each other again. Stop before the child gets tired.

Level 5 Characteristics

- Says name
- Demanding
- Volatile emotions
- Commands supervision when with others same age
- Shares with supervision
- Frustrated by restrictions
- A lot of interaction with other children (but little cooperation between them)
- Play includes hitting and pushing
- Needs help to resolve problems
- Repeats sounds or words
- Difficulty making choices and sticking with them
- Tiptoes
- Throws and kicks ball
- Runs with falling
- Has at least a 50 word vocabulary
- Imitates
- Follows 2-step command
- Able to take things apart
- 2 minute attention span
- Likes being read to
- Initiation and usual completion of potty training
- Starts using "toilet" words

Level 5 Information

Self-esteem is a feeling.
If you have HIGH self-esteem...
>   You make good friends!
>   You care about yourself and other people;
>   You are responsible;
>   You enjoy learning;
>   You are proud of what you do;
>   You can handle failure;
>   You can share feelings.

HIGH self-esteem is having a GOOD feeling about yourself, your place in the family, your school, and your world.

THINGS TO REMEMBER:

- At the end of the activity, PRAISE the child (give a hug!).
- Be GENTLE when you tell the child about something they did not do right.
- If the child is trying, but still not getting it right, just say "Nice try!"...and TRY AGAIN.
- There is no right or wrong with these activities. NO ONE FAILS! YOU DO NOT FAIL if the child cannot or will not do it...and the CHILD DOES NOT FAIL!
- Set a bed time that is the same every night. Let the child choose if they want a nightlight.
- Look for the Good Stuff!
- Do not use foul language in front of the child.
- PRAISE sharing.
- Children take things in their life VERY seriously. You should too. It shows RESPECT for the child.
- Keep adult sexual activity private.
- FIND A REASON TO SAY EACH OF THESE PHRASES ONCE A DAY:
  Good work!
  That's the right way to do it!
  Terrific!

DON'T GIVE UP!

— If the child does not want to do the activity with you the way you want him or her to...try again tomorrow.
— Keep trying. This is the way you **SHOW** the child that you mean what you say. A child needs to **TRUST** in order to share with you or listen to you.
— **HOW** you say something is sometimes more important than **WHAT** you say.

You may be doing MOST of these things already as part of the way you care for children and run your home. By doing these things in the way they are written, you will be helping the child's self-esteem **plus** your own self-esteem.

When you can help somebody feel good...
you feel good!

"I" messages let the child know exactly what you want, why you want it, and how you want it. The child does not have to GUESS what you want or how you feel. This is a way of setting LIMITS. Some examples are:

- **"I** feel very upset when you throw your clothes on the floor. Clothes cost money... **I** work hard for my money and **I** want you to have nice clothes to wear."
- **"I** do not want you to carry those two full glasses of milk at one time. **I** am afraid they will spill."

The BASE program is about helping children have HIGH self-esteem. It is a group of things to do and share with a child. These things are short, simple and positive. They should be done everyday when possible.

REMEMBER:

If any of these things do not agree with the way you believe or your religion (example: dancing), do not do it.

Level 5 Human Awareness

Here are some things for you to talk about with your child. It means a lot for you to let the child know that you want to talk about these things.

BOTH PARENTS SHOULD PARTICIPATE. When possible, both parents should share the responsibility for sex education. Men have expected most sex education to be done by the mother. When both parents participate, the child sees sex education as a family affair.

What you should say when the child asks you something:

Always answer. Do not wait to tell what he or she wants to know, even if it seems that he or she is asking in order to shock you. Do not say, "I'll tell you when you are older". Answer in the right way and with good information for the child's age. You build self-esteem when you answer. If you *do not* tell what he or she wants to know, the child learns: 1. not to ask you things; or, 2. that he or she is not "big" enough or "good" enough.

The genitals are sometimes called the "private parts" of the body. In a child, they are at the bottom of the body. Use the right names when you talk about the genitals.

If the child is touching his or her private parts when with other people or out of the house you should:

1. Try to get him or her to think about something else by talking to him or her, showing him or her something, and so on;

2. Do not try to do something about it right then. Do not make a big deal about it. Do not put the child down.
3. Later, when you are at home with him or her and no one is with you, say "It's okay to touch yourself there, but that is something we do not do when others are around."

If he or she asks you where a baby comes from, say: "There is a special place between Mommy's legs that the baby comes out of."

Teaching about sex cannot be done at one time. When the child asks questions, they must be answered at all ages. Let him or her know that it is okay to ask questions. Tell the truth when you answer. This helps you to get ready to deal with what comes up when he or she is a teenager.

If the child talks about things that make you think he or she may have been sexually abused, contact your pediatrician, clinic, or phone a child abuse hotline.

When the child asks questions that you don't have answers for, ask your family doctor, clinic, or health department.

REMEMBER:
If anything written here is against your religious or moral beliefs, don't do it!

❏ *Approval* ❏ *Sense of Power* ❏ *Acceptance*

● **SPEND SOME TIME TALKING WITH THE CHILD. WHEN HE OR SHE SAYS SOMETHING, SAY SOMETHING BACK.**

1. When you are with the child, be sure to listen to what he or she is saying.
2. If he or she says something, even if it is only one word, say something back. When playing with toys, he or she may say "mine". You could then say, "Yes, those are your toys. I have some more over here. They are mine, but I'll give them to you."
3. If the child does not talk much, look at pictures in magazines or books. Point to things and name them, like "pretty kitty". Give him or her a chance to say what you said. Name things in the room, like "chair, table, door".
4. A toy phone is good for a child to use. Play that you are talking to the child. Hold your hand to your ear like when you are on a real phone. The child may say "hello" into the phone. You can say something like, "I would like you to come and play with me".

❏ *Approval* ❏ *Trust* ❏ *Acceptance*

● **THE CHILD WILL LEARN THE NAMES FOR PARTS OF HIS OR HER BODY WHEN YOU PLAY GAMES WITH HIM OR HER.**

1. Pick out 3 body parts each day—hand, elbow, knee, nose, ear, finger, eye, ankle, back, or any others.
2. Play the game, "I'm going to get your nose" or "I'm going to kiss your ear". Be sure to use the 3 body parts you picked for the day.
3. Games should be played by gently touching the parts of the body. No tickling or pinching.
4. Have him or her "get" your nose or ear. Tell him or her you like how **gentle** he or she is being.

❏ *Approval* ❏ *Sense of Power* ❏ *Acceptance* ❏ *Responsibility* ❏ *Pride*

● **THE CHILD SHOULD PRACTICE POURING.**

1. Put a little juice, milk, or water in a small pitcher, small milk carton, or small measuring cup.
2. Let the child pour the juice or milk into his or her cup or bowl. Help the first 1 or 2 times.
3. Tell that you like the way he or she is learning to pour. Have him or her keep trying to pour at different times.
4. Let the child pour other things into a large bowl

when you are cooking, making jello, or baking.
5. Praise the child for doing a good job.
6. In front of the child, tell another adult that he or she "did such a good job."

❏ *Approval* ❏ *Sense of Power* ❏ *Acceptance* ❏ *Responsibility*

● **CHILDREN LIKE TO PLAY THAT THEY ARE THE "MOMMY" OR "DADDY".**

1. Show the child a stuffed toy or doll.
2. If he or she wants to act like "Mommy" or "Daddy", tell him or her that it is nice to play that way.
3. The child may want *you* to be the baby when you are playing. This is okay.
4. Show the child the way to love the doll or stuffed toy by hugging and being nice. (Nice touching.)

❏ *Approval* ❏ *Sense of Power* ❏ *Acceptance* ❏ *Responsibility*

● **CHILDREN LIKE TO DRESS UP IN MOMMY'S OR DADDY'S CLOTHES.**

1. Give the child 2 to 3 more objects that he or she can keep in a toy box. Examples: purses, hats, jewelry, skirts, blouses, shirts, ties, or shoes. If the child does not have his or her own dress-up things, let him or her know which clothes of yours can be used and which are not to be touched.
2. If the child "dresses up", tell him or her how nice he or she looks. A girl or boy may dress as a woman or man. This is okay. It may just look like fun to a boy to wear high heels or to a girl to wear men's big shoes.
3. Praise the child for being *so* big.

❏ *Pride*

● **DANCING WITH A CHILD TO MUSIC IS A GOOD ACTIVITY AND CAN BE FUN (3 minutes).**

1. Turn on some music—radio, record, tape.
2. Hold the child's hands with your two hands and dance.
3. Little children can be picked up in your arms while you dance to music.
4. When dancing to slow music you can hold each other closely.
5. Tell the child how much you like to dance with him or her.
6. Stop dancing before the child gets too excited. Try to end using slow music.

❏ *Approval* ❏ *Sense of Power* ❏ *Acceptance*
❏ *Responsibility* ❏ *Self-respect* ❏ *Pride*

● **HELP THE CHILD MAKE HIS OR HER OWN PICTURE BOOK OR SCRAPBOOK. Parents, this does not cost money. You can make your own book. Make a hole on the side of 6 to 10 sheets of paper. Push a string or ribbon through the holes and tie a bow.**

1. Let the child talk about things he or she would like in the picture book; balls, favorite food, pets, playing on a playground, etc.
2. Try to find pictures for the picture book in magazines and newspapers.
3. If the child can use a child's scissors with **rounded ends,** let him or her cut out the picture. **Do not leave him or her alone with the scissors**. You may cut out the picture if the child cannot.
4. Let him or her paste the picture on the paper of the book.
5. Have the child show other people the book and have him or her tell about it.
6. Praise him or her for the nice book.

❏ *Approval* ❏ *Sense of Power* ❏ *Acceptance*

● **SPEND SOME TIME TALKING WITH THE CHILD. WHEN HE OR SHE SAYS SOMETHING, SAY SOMETHING BACK.**

1. When you are with the child, be sure to listen to what he or she is saying.
2. If he or she says something, even if it is only one word, say something back. When playing with toys, he or she may say "mine". You could then say, "Yes, those are your toys. I have some more over here. They are mine, but I'll give them to you."
3. If the child does not talk much, look at pictures in magazines or books. Point to things and name them, like "pretty kitty". Give him or her a chance to say what you said. Name things in the room, like "chair, table, door".
4. A toy phone is good for a child to use. Play that you are talking to the child. Hold your hand to your ear like when you are on a real phone. The child may say "hello" into the phone. You can say something like, "I would like you to come and play with me".

❏ *Approval* ❏ *Trust* ❏ *Acceptance*

● **THE CHILD WILL LEARN THE NAMES FOR PARTS OF HIS OR HER BODY WHEN YOU PLAY GAMES WITH HIM OR HER.**

1. Pick out 3 body parts each day—hand, elbow, knee, nose, ear, finger, eye, ankle, back, or any others.
2. Play the game, "I'm going to get your nose" or "I'm going to kiss your ear". Be sure to use the 3 body parts you picked for the day.
3. Games should be played by gently touching the parts of the body. No tickling or pinching.
4. Have him or her "get" your nose or ear. Tell him or her you like how **gentle** he or she is being.

❏ *Approval* ❏ *Sense of Power* ❏ *Acceptance* ❏ *Responsibility*

● **READ A BOOK OR LOOK THROUGH A MAGAZINE TOGETHER.**

1. Find a special place to keep the child's books, maybe in the bedroom.
2. Read to the child in a quiet place—no TV or radio on.
3. Show the child 2 or 3 books. Let him or her pick the one you should read.
4. Sit close to the child while reading so that you touch each other. Let the child turn the pages when he or she wants to. It is okay if he or she

turns a few pages at a time.
5. If the child points to a picture, tell him or her that you like that.
6. Some children may be ready for a trip to the library to pick out their own books. Do not push the child to do this if he or she doesn't want to go.
7. When reading a story change the sound of your voice when you read about different people. Let the child do this, too. Make noises about things you're reading about—like dogs, "Bow-wow."
8. If the child wants to play like he or she is reading the story to you, it is okay.
9. It is okay if the child wants to read the same book every day.

❏ *Approval* ❏ *Sense of Power* ❏ *Acceptance* ❏ *Responsibility* ❏ *Pride*

● **LET THE CHILD DRAW SOMETIMES WHEN YOU ARE TOGETHER AND HE OR SHE IS PLAYING.**

1. Use a large piece of paper, grocery sack, or newspaper opened up.
2. Use two crayons.
3. Put the paper on the floor or a table so the child can reach and draw on it easily.
4. Show how to hold the crayon.
5. You can draw a line with a crayon. The child can draw lines, circles, or anything with the crayon.
6. Let him or her draw anything, but tell him or her to stay on the paper.
7. Stop when the child wants to. Tell him or her that you like the drawing. Praise the child's work. "What a beautiful picture you drew."
8. Have him or her help you put the picture on the refrigerator using tape.

❏ *Approval* ❏ *Sense of Power* ❏ *Acceptance* ❏ *Self-respect* ❏ *Pride*

● **RUNNING OUTSIDE IS GOOD FOR THE CHILD AND CAN BE FUN!**

1. Pick a place where you have space to run.
2. Get the child to run with you.
3. Say "I can catch you." Then run to him or her, give a hug and step back.
4. Say: "I bet you can't catch me." Run slowly so he or she does catch you.
5. Tell him or her that he or she can run fast. "Good job."
6. Play game 2 or 3 times, then do something quieter like watching clouds or planes.
7. At the end of game, give child a big hug.

Level 5

❏ *Approval* ❏ *Sense of Power* ❏ *Acceptance*
❏ *Responsibility* ❏ *Self-respect* ❏ *Pride*

● **HELP THE CHILD MAKE HIS OR HER OWN PICTURE BOOK OR SCRAPBOOK. Parents, this does not cost money. You can make your own book. Make a hole on the side of 6 to 10 sheets of paper. Push a string or ribbon through the holes and tie a bow.**

1. Let the child talk about things he or she would like in the picture book; balls, favorite food, pets, playing on a playground, etc.
2. Try to find pictures for the picture book in magazines and newspapers.
3. If the child can use a child's scissors with **rounded ends,** let him or her cut out the picture. **Do not leave him or her alone with the scissors**. You may cut out the picture if the child cannot.
4. Let him or her paste the picture on the paper of the book.
5. Have the child show other people the book and have him or her tell about it.
6. Praise him or her for the nice book.

❏ *Approval* ❏ *Sense of Power* ❏ *Acceptance*

● **SPEND SOME TIME TALKING WITH THE CHILD. WHEN HE OR SHE SAYS SOMETHING, SAY SOMETHING BACK.**

1. When you are with the child, be sure to listen to what he or she is saying.
2. If he or she says something, even if it is only one word, say something back. When playing with toys, he or she may say "mine". You could then say, "Yes, those are your toys. I have some more over here. They are mine, but I'll give them to you."
3. If the child does not talk much, look at pictures in magazines or books. Point to things and name them, like "pretty kitty". Give him or her a chance to say what you said. Name things in the room, like "chair, table, door".
4. A toy phone is good for a child to use. Play that you are talking to the child. Hold your hand to your ear like when you are on a real phone. The child may say "hello" into the phone. You can say something like, "I would like you to come and play with me".

❏ *Approval* ❏ *Sense of Power*
❏ *Acceptance* ❏ *Responsibility*

● **READ A BOOK OR LOOK THROUGH A MAGAZINE TOGETHER.**

1. Find a special place to keep the child's books.
2. Read to the child in a quiet place—no TV or radio on.
3. Show the child 2 or 3 books. Let him or her pick the one you should read.
4. Sit close to the child while reading so that you touch each other. Let the child turn the pages when he or she wants to. It is okay if he or she turns a few pages at a time.
5. If the child points to a picture, tell him or her that you like that.
6. Some children may be ready for a trip to the library to pick out their own books. Do not push the child to do this if he or she doesn't want to go.
7. When reading a story change the sound of your voice when you read about different people. Let the child do this, too. Make noises about things you're reading about—like dogs, "Bow-wow,"
8. If the child wants to play like he or she is reading the story to you, it is okay.
9. It is okay if the child wants to read the same book every day.

Level 5

❏ *Approval* ❏ *Sense of Power*
❏ *Acceptance* ❏ *Responsibility* ❏ *Pride*

● **LET THE CHILD DRAW SOMETIMES WHEN YOU ARE TOGETHER AND HE OR SHE IS PLAYING.**

1. Use a large piece of paper, grocery sack, or newspaper opened up.
2. Use two crayons.
3. Put the paper on the floor or a table so the child can reach and draw on it easily.
4. Show how to hold the crayon.
5. You can draw a line with a crayon. The child can draw lines, circles, or anything with the crayon.
6. Let him or her draw anything, but tell him or her to stay on the paper.
7. Stop when the child wants to. Tell him or her that you like the drawing. Praise the child's work. "What a beautiful picture you drew."
8. Have him or her help you put the picture on the refrigerator using tape.

❏ *Approval* ❏ *Acceptance*

● **FOR A FEW MINUTES DURING PLAYTIME, YOU CAN BE WITH THE CHILD AND MAKE THE NOISE OF ANIMALS OR OTHER THINGS. THIS IS A GOOD, QUIET KIND OF GAME.**

1. Think of sounds that the child knows, such as mewing, barking, mooing like a cow. Make the sound in a soft, playful way and ask, "Who is that?"
2. Let the child make sounds for you to guess. Sometimes play that you can't guess.
3. If the child does some sounds try to make noises of harder things like an airplane, duck, sheep. Let him or her guess.
4. Go around the house with the child. Find things that make a noise and let him or her hear them.

❏ *Pride*

● **DANCING WITH A CHILD TO MUSIC IS A GOOD ACTIVITY AND CAN BE FUN (3 minutes).**

1. Turn on some music—radio, record, tape.
2. Hold the child's hands with your two hands and dance.
3. Little children can be picked up in your arms while you dance to music.
4. When dancing to slow music you can hold each other closely.
5. Tell the child how much you like to dance with him or her.
6. Stop dancing before the child gets too excited. Try to end using slow music.

3-4 years

Level 6 Characteristics

- Delightful
- Capacity to build trust in important adults
- Takes stairs one foot at a time
- Cooperative play
- Imaginary playmates
- Accepts things easier
- Says 3 to 4 word sentences
- Will share and take turns
- Able to ride a tricycle
- Follows a 3-step command
- Has concept of self and gender
- Able to stand on one foot
- Nap may become optional
- Likes to please
- Tests authority (checking limits)
- Control of emotions beginning to emerge
- Friends are important (social interchange)
- Silly
- Coordination becoming more refined
- Repeats initial sounds
- Practices different roles
- Becoming interested in rules
- Increasing attention span
- Beginning to ask and answer questions
- Night terrors
- Creative play
- Beginning to pretend
- With guidance, can focus on shape, color, and size

Level 6 Information

Self-esteem is a feeling.

If you have HIGH self-esteem...

> You make good friends!
> You care about yourself and other people;
> You are responsible;
> You enjoy learning;
> You are proud of what you do;
> You can handle failure;
> You can share feelings.

HIGH self-esteem is having a GOOD feeling about yourself, your place in the family, your school, and your world.

THINGS TO REMEMBER:

- Do not walk around the house nude.
- Do not use foul language in front of the child.
- Set a bed time and bath time that is the same every night.
- Keep adult sexual activity private.
- When the child does something GOOD...tell him or her.
- Look for the Good Stuff and PRAISE the child for it!
- FIND A REASON TO SAY EACH OF THESE PHRASES ONCE A DAY:
  Now you have it!
  Fantastic!
  I like that!

DON'T GIVE UP!

— If the child does not want to do the activity with you the way you want him or her to...try again tomorrow.

— Keep trying. This is the way you SHOW the child that you mean what you say. A child needs to TRUST in order to share with you or listen to you.

— HOW you say something is sometimes more important than WHAT you say.

You may be doing MOST of these things already as part of the way you care for children and run your home. By doing these things in the way they are written, you will be helping the child's self-esteem **plus** your own self-esteem.

When you can help somebody feel good... you feel good!

"I" messages let the child know exactly what you want, why you want it, and how you want it. The child does not have to GUESS what you want or how you feel. This is a way of setting LIMITS. Some examples are:

- "**I** feel very upset when you throw your clothes on the floor. Clothes cost money... **I** work hard for my money and **I** want you to have nice clothes to wear."
- "**I** do not want you to carry those two full glasses of milk at one time. **I** am afraid they will spill."

The BASE program is about helping children have HIGH self-esteem. It is a group of things to do and share with a child. These things are short, simple and positive. They should be done everyday when possible.

REMEMBER:

If any of these things do not agree with the way you believe or your religion (example: dancing), do not do it.

Level 6 Human Awareness

Here are some things for you to talk about with your child. It means a lot for you to let the child know that you want to talk about these things.

BOTH PARENTS SHOULD PARTICIPATE. When possible, both parents should share the responsibility for sex education. Men have expected most sex education to be done by the mother. When both parents participate, the child sces sex education as a family affair.

How to get the child to ask questions:

Listen to what he or she talks about and when the time is right tell him or her some things. The child may tell you about how many puppies the dog next door had. Then you may say, "Yes, dogs have more children at a time than people do. We have one or two babies at a time." This gives him or her a chance to ask more questions.

What you should say when the child asks you something:

Always answer. Do not wait to tell what he or she wants to know, even if it seems that he or she is asking in order to shock you. Do not say, "I'll tell you when you are older". Answer in the right way and with good information for the child's age. You build self-esteem when you answer. If you *do not* tell what he or she wants to know, the child learns: 1. not to ask you things; or, 2. that he or she is not "big" enough or "good" enough.

The genitals are sometimes called the "private parts" of the body. In a child, they are at the bottom of the body. Use the right names when you talk about the genitals.

If the child is touching his or her private parts when with other people or out of the house you should:
1. Try to get him or her to think about something else by talking to him or her, showing him or her something, and so on;
2. Do not try to do something about it right then. Do not make a big deal about it. Do not put the child down.
3. Later, when you are at home with him or her and no one is with you, say "It's okay to touch yourself there, but that is something we do not do when others are around."

If he or she asks you where a baby comes from, say: "There is a special place between Mommy's legs that the baby comes out of."

Teaching about sex cannot be done at one time. When the child asks questions, they must be answered at all ages. Let him or her know that it is okay to ask questions. Tell the truth when you answer. This helps you to get ready to deal with what comes up when he or she is a teenager.

If the child talks about things that make you think he or she may have been sexually abused, contact your pediatrician, clinic, or phone a child abuse hotline.

When the child asks questions that you don't have answers for, ask your family doctor, clinic, or health department.

REMEMBER:
If anything written here is against your religious or moral beliefs, don't do it!

❏ *Approval* ❏ *Sense of Power*
❏ *Acceptance* ❏ *Pride*

● **WHEN THE CHILD DRAWS A PICTURE, PUT IT WHERE EVERYONE CAN SEE IT. TELL HIM OR HER WHAT A NICE PICTURE HE OR SHE DREW.**

1. Have a place for the child's pictures. Put them on your wall, door, or refrigerator.
2. When he or she brings a picture made in church school or day care, put it up right away. Leave it up for one week.
3. Tell others in the family that you think the picture is nice, you like the colors, or anything else that is good.
4. If the child does not have a chance to draw somewhere else, help him or her make a picture at home every week.
5. Whatever he or she draws is okay. Ask him or her to tell you about the picture.

❏ *Approval* ❏ *Sense of Power* ❏ *Pride*

● **TALK WITH THE CHILD ABOUT HIS OR HER GOOD FRIENDS AND HOW THEY PLAY TOGETHER.**

1. Pick a time to talk when no one else is there and you do not have to hurry.
2. Ask him or her to tell you about his or her best friend and ask about other friends as well.
3. "Did you play together today?" "What did you do or what did you play?"
4. "What do you like best about your friend?"
5. "What is a friend?" Talk about what a friend is and how to be a friend to someone.

❏ *Trust* ❏ *Acceptance* ❏ *Responsibility*

● **GIVE THE CHILD A *RESPONSIBILITY* INSTEAD OF CALLING THE "JOB" A CHORE.**

1. Pick something that he or she can do as part of the job *with* you. (Putting on napkins while Mom or Dad sets the table. Folding dishtowels while you fold the rest of the laundry.)
2. Make this a part of what you do together each day.
3. Be sure to tell your child each time how pleased you are that he or she can take this responsibility. (Use the word **responsibility**.) Tell how important it is that everyone has their own place in the family and their own responsibilities to the family.

❏ *Approval* ❏ *Trust* ❏ *Acceptance*

● **A CHILD MAY LEARN TO TRUST SOMEONE WHEN THEY ARE TOUCHED BY THEM.**

1. If the child does not want to be hugged or touched, do not force him or her.
2. Let the child know that you do care about him or her. Try to show this by the way you act at different times.
3. A gentle pat or touch on the head will be okay with him or her. This may help the child to learn to like being touched so that later, he or she will like a more loving kind of touch.

❏ *Approval* ❏ *Acceptance* ❏ *Pride*

● **IT IS FUN TO TELL SOMEBODY SOMETHING YOU LIKE ABOUT THEM OR LIKE ABOUT SOMETHING THEY DO; OR FOR SOMEONE TO DO THE SAME FOR YOU. THIS IS GIVING AND TAKING A COMPLIMENT.**

1. You say: "I'm going to tell you something I like about you or about something you do!" Then tell the child something that he or she did. Example: "You brushed your teeth so well today," or "I liked the way you shared your toys with your friends."
2. Ask him or her to give you a compliment.
3. Give compliments two more times.

❏ *Approval* ❏ *Acceptance* ❏ *Pride*

● **WHEN YOU SEE THE CHILD DOING SOMETHING THAT IS GOOD BE SURE TO TELL HIM OR HER THAT YOU LIKE THAT.**

"You did such a good job getting dressed!"
"I like the way you smile when you see me!"
"You were so gentle with the baby!"
"I like the way you share with your brother/sister!"

❏ *Acceptance*

● **SING A SONG TOGETHER (Clap hands two times at the end of each line).**

1. If you're happy and you know it clap your hands.
   If you're happy and you know it clap your hands.
   If you're happy and you know it then your life will surely show it...
   If you're happy and you know it (and so on—just change the thing you do):
      stamp your feet
      raise your arms

(continued...)

shake your head
wave hello
or any other thing you want to do.

2. When you say what to do, give him or her time to say it or to say the next part. If he or she does not go on with the song, you should sing it.
3. Do this together.
4. Show that you are having a good time by smiling. Praise him or her for following directions (what you do) so well. Be sure to tell him or her which directions he or she followed so well.

❐ *Trust* ❐ *Acceptance*

● **HELP THE CHILD TO LEARN WHICH SEX HE OR SHE IS (3-4 minutes).**

1. Ask, "Are you a boy or a girl?" If he or she does not know, tell him or her.
2. Have him or her look through a magazine or picture book and show you pictures of boys or girls.
3. Use the right names—boy, girl, man, woman.
4. Be sure to tell that boys grow up to be men and girls grow up to be women.

❐ *Trust*

● **TALK WITH THE CHILD ABOUT FAMILIES.**

1. Meal time may be a good time to talk.
2. Things you want the child to know:
   A. Families may be made up in different ways. There may be only a father or a mother. A family may have grandparents, aunts, cousins, and so on. A family may be a stepfather or stepmother with children, so there are stepbrothers and stepsisters.
   B. No one kind of family is best. All kinds can be okay.
   C. Every family has different rules, and that's okay. No one set of rules is best or right. Everyone in the family must live by their family rules.
3. Ways to help the child when he or she says something about the different ones in the family.
   A. Everyone in the family can be different and have different things happen in their life. This is okay.
   B. You should not say that one child is better than the other in any way. They may be different, but don't let them get the feeling that he or she is better or not as good.

❏ *Approval* ❏ *Sense of Power*
❏ *Acceptance* ❏ *Pride*

● **WHEN THE CHILD DRAWS A PICTURE, PUT IT WHERE EVERYONE CAN SEE IT. TELL HIM OR HER WHAT A NICE PICTURE HE OR SHE DREW.**

1. Have a place for the child's pictures. Put them on your wall, door, or refrigerator.
2. When he or she brings a picture made in church school or day care, put it up right away. Leave it up for one week.
3. Tell others in the family that you think the picture is nice, you like the colors, or anything else that is good.
4. If the child does not have a chance to draw somewhere else, help him or her make a picture at home every week.
5. Whatever he or she draws is okay. Ask him or her to tell you about the picture.

❏ *Approval* ❏ *Sense of Power* ❏ *Pride*

● **TALK WITH THE CHILD ABOUT HIS OR HER GOOD FRIENDS AND HOW THEY PLAY TOGETHER.**

1. Pick a time to talk when no one else is there and you do not have to hurry.
2. Ask him or her to tell you about his or her best friend and ask about other friends as well.
3. "Did you play together today?" "What did you do or what did you play?"
4. "What do you like best about your friend?"
5. "What is a friend?" Talk about what a friend is and how to be a friend to someone.

❏ *Trust* ❏ *Acceptance* ❏ *Responsibility*

● **GIVE THE CHILD A *RESPONSIBILITY* INSTEAD OF CALLING THE "JOB" A CHORE.**

1. Pick something that he or she can do as part of the job *with* you. (Putting on napkins while Mom or Dad sets the table. Folding dishtowels while you fold the rest of the laundry.)
2. Make this a part of what you do together each day.
3. Be sure to tell your child each time how pleased you are that he or she can take this responsibility. (Use the word **responsibility**.) Tell how important it is that everyone has their own place in the family and their own responsibilities to the family.

❏ *Approval* ❏ *Trust* ❏ *Acceptance*

● **A CHILD MAY LEARN TO TRUST SOMEONE WHEN THEY ARE TOUCHED BY THEM.**

1. If the child does not want to be hugged or touched, do not force him or her.
2. Let the child know that you do care about him or her. Try to show this by the way you act at different times.
3. A gentle pat or touch on the head will be okay with him or her. This may help the child to learn to like being touched so that later, he or she will like a more loving kind of touch.

❏ *Approval* ❏ *Acceptance* ❏ *Pride*

● **IT IS FUN TO TELL SOMEBODY SOMETHING YOU LIKE ABOUT THEM OR LIKE ABOUT SOMETHING THEY DO; OR FOR SOMEONE TO DO THE SAME FOR YOU. THIS IS GIVING AND TAKING A COMPLIMENT.**

1. You say: "I'm going to tell you something I like about you or about something you do!" Then tell the child something that he or she did. Example: "You brushed your teeth so well today," or "I liked the way you shared your toys with your friends."
2. Ask him or her to give you a compliment.
3. Give compliments two more times.

❏ *Approval* ❏ *Acceptance* ❏ *Pride*

● **WHEN YOU SEE THE CHILD DOING SOMETHING THAT IS GOOD BE SURE TO TELL HIM OR HER THAT YOU LIKE THAT.**

"You did such a good job getting dressed!"
"I like the way you smile when you see me!"
"You were so gentle with the baby!"
"I like the way you share with your brother/sister!"

◻ *Acceptance*

● **SING A SONG TOGETHER (Clap hands two times at the end of each line).**

1. If you're happy and you know it clap your hands.
   If you're happy and you know it clap your hands.
   If you're happy and you know it then your life will surely show it...
   If you're happy and you know it (and so on— just change the thing you do):
   > stamp your feet
   > raise your arms
   > shake your head
   > wave hello
   > or any other thing you want to do.

2. When you say what to do, give him or her time to say it or to say the next part. If he or she does not go on with the song, you should sing it.

3. Do this together.

4. Show that you are having a good time by smiling. Praise him or her for following directions (what you do) so well. Be sure to tell him or her which directions he or she followed so well.

❐ *Approval* ❐ *Sense of Power*
❐ *Acceptance* ❐ *Pride*

● **WHEN THE CHILD DRAWS A PICTURE, PUT IT WHERE EVERYONE CAN SEE IT. TELL HIM OR HER WHAT A NICE PICTURE HE OR SHE DREW.**

1. Have a place for the child's pictures. Put them on your wall, door, or refrigerator.
2. When he or she brings a picture made in church school or day care, put it up right away. Leave it up for one week.
3. Tell others in the family that you think the picture is nice, you like the colors, or anything else that is good.
4. If the child does not have a chance to draw somewhere else, help him or her make a picture at home every week.
5. Whatever he or she draws is okay. Ask him or her to tell you about the picture.

❐ *Approval* ❐ *Sense of Power*
❐ *Acceptance* ❐ *Pride*

● **YOU AND THE CHILD SHOULD WORK OUT SOME ACTION OR SIGN THAT YOU DO WITH EACH OTHER AS SOMETHING SPECIAL.**

1. You may blow kisses, wink, "high five," or any other action that you work out.
2. Let the child do the action or sign first sometimes, then you do it back to him or her.
3. Say that you feel good when he or she shares this with you.

❐ *Approval* ❐ *Acceptance* ❐ *Pride*

● **IT IS FUN TO TELL SOMEBODY SOMETHING YOU LIKE ABOUT THEM OR LIKE ABOUT SOMETHING THEY DO; OR FOR SOMEONE TO DO THE SAME FOR YOU. THIS IS GIVING AND TAKING A COMPLIMENT.**

1. You say: "I'm going to tell you something I like about you or about something you do!" Then tell the child something that he or she did. Example: "You brushed your teeth so well today," or "I liked the way you shared your toys with your friends."
2. Ask him or her to give you a compliment.
3. Give compliments two more times.

❐ *Approval* ❐ *Acceptance* ❐ *Pride*

● **WHEN YOU SEE THE CHILD DOING SOMETHING THAT IS GOOD BE SURE TO TELL HIM OR HER THAT YOU LIKE THAT.**

"You did such a good job getting dressed!"
"I like the way you smile when you see me!"
"You were so gentle with the baby!"
"I like the way you share with your brother/sister!"

❏ *Acceptance*

● **SING A SONG TOGETHER (Clap hands two times at the end of each line).**

1. If you're happy and you know it clap your hands.
   If you're happy and you know it clap your hands.
   If you're happy and you know it then your life will surely show it...
   If you're happy and you know it (and so on—just change the thing you do):
   >stamp your feet
   >raise your arms
   >shake your head
   >wave hello
   >or any other thing you want to do.
2. When you say what to do, give him or her time to say it or to say the next part. If he or she does not go on with the song, you should sing it.
3. Do this together.
4. Show that you are having a good time by smiling. Praise him or her for following directions (what you do) so well. Be sure to tell him or her which directions he or she followed so well.

❏ *Approval* ❏ *Sense of Power*
❏ *Acceptance* ❏ *Pride*

● **YOU AND THE CHILD SHOULD WORK OUT SOME ACTION OR SIGN THAT YOU DO WITH EACH OTHER AS SOMETHING SPECIAL.**

1. You may blow kisses, wink, "high five," or any other action that you work out.
2. Let the child do the action or sign first sometimes, then you do it back to him or her.
3. Say that you feel good when he or she shares this with you.

❏ *Approval* ❏ *Acceptance* ❏ *Pride*

● **WHEN YOU SEE THE CHILD DOING SOMETHING THAT IS GOOD BE SURE TO TELL HIM OR HER THAT YOU LIKE THAT.**

"You did such a good job getting dressed!"
"I like the way you smile when you see me!"
"You were so gentle with the baby!"
"I like the way you share with your brother/sister!"

4-5 years

Level 7 Characteristics

- Energetic
- Experiments (will try different foods, will try to put things together and take apart)
- Adventurous (child less clingy, jumps from trees)
- Understands limits
- Occasionally may kick/hit/spit
- Moves quickly from laughter to tears and vice-versa
- Not able to separate fact from fantasy
- Name calling
- Unpredictable
- Self-motivating
- Constructive play
- Has super heroes
- Able to cope with frustration
- Begins asking questions about himself or herself—"Where do I come from?"
- Bad dreams
- Modest
- Cautious
- Recites nursery rhymes
- Likes to play with other children and has special friends
- Sometimes brags

Level 7 Information

Self-esteem is a feeling.

If you have HIGH self-esteem...
- You make good friends!
- You care about yourself and other people;
- You are responsible;
- You enjoy learning;
- You are proud of what you do;
- You can handle failure;
- You can share feelings.

HIGH self-esteem is having a GOOD feeling about yourself, your place in the family, your school, and your world.

THINGS TO REMEMBER:

- Call the child by name (ask the child if he or she likes to be called by another name or nickname).
- Play should be nice touching. No hitting or spitting.
- If the child does not play nicely...have him or her "sit out" (move away from the action) for 3 to 4 minutes.
- If the child uses a curse word, suggest a "better" word use.
- DO NOT use foul language in front of the child.
- DO NOT walk around the house nude.
- Keep adult sexual activity private.
- ORDER THE DAY'S ACTIVITIES! "Today is Monday, June 15."
- Talk about what the day is going to be like so that the child knows what to expect.
- Talk about things that are planned for the day, and when they are planned to happen.
- Let the child know YOUR plans for the day, so that he or she will know where you are if he or she needs you.
- FIND A REASON TO SAY EACH OF THESE PHRASES ONCE A DAY: That's the way to do it! Good remembering!

DON'T GIVE UP!

— If the child does not want to do the activity with you the way you want him or her to...try again tomorrow.

— Keep trying. This is the way you **SHOW** the child that you mean what you say. A child needs to **TRUST** in order to share with you or listen to you.

— **HOW** you say something is sometimes more important than **WHAT** you say.

You may be doing MOST of these things already as part of the way you care for children and run your home. By doing these things in the way they are written, you will be helping the child's self-esteem **plus** your own self-esteem.

When you can help somebody feel good... you feel good!

"I" messages let the child know exactly what you want, why you want it, and how you want it. The child does not have to GUESS what you want or how you feel. This is a way of setting LIMITS. Some examples are:

- **"I** feel very upset when you throw your clothes on the floor. Clothes cost money... **I** work hard for my money and **I** want you to have nice clothes to wear."
- **"I** do not want you to carry those two full glasses of milk at one time. **I** am afraid they will spill."

The BASE program is about helping children have HIGH self-esteem. It is a group of things to do and share with a child. These things are short, simple and positive. They should be done everyday when possible.

REMEMBER:

If any of these things do not agree with the way you believe or your religion (example: dancing), do not do it.

Level 7 Human Awareness

Here are some things for you to talk about with your child. It means a lot for you to let the child know that you want to talk about these things.

BOTH PARENTS SHOULD PARTICIPATE. When possible, both parents should share the responsibility for sex education. Men have expected most sex education to be done by the mother. When both parents participate, the child sees sex education as a family affair.

How to get the child to ask questions:

Listen to what he or she talks about and when the time is right tell him or her some things. The child may tell you about how many puppies the dog next door had. Then you may say, "Yes, dogs have more children at a time than people do. We have one or two babies at a time." This gives him or her a chance to ask more questions.

What you should say when the child asks you something:

Always answer. Do not wait to tell what he or she wants to know, even if it seems that he or she is asking in order to shock you. Do not say, "I'll tell you when you are older". Answer in the right way and with good information for the child's age. You build self-esteem when you answer. If you *do not* tell what he or she wants to know, the child learns: 1. not to ask you things; or, 2. that he or she is not "big" enough or "good" enough.

The genitals are sometimes called the "private parts" of the body. In a child, they are at the bottom of the body. Use the right names when you talk about the genitals.

If the child is touching his or her private parts when with other people or out of the house you should:

1. Try to get him or her to think about something else by talking to him or her, showing him or her something, and so on;
2. Do not try to do something about it right then. Do not make a big deal about it. Do not put the child down.
3. Later, when you are at home with him or her and no one is with you, say "It's okay to touch yourself there, but that is something we do not do when others are around."

If he or she asks you where a baby comes from, say. "There is a special place between Mommy's legs that the baby comes out of".

Teaching about sex cannot be done at one time. When the child asks questions, they must be answered at all ages. Let him or her know that it is okay to ask questions. Tell the truth when you answer. This helps you to get ready to deal with what comes up when he or she is a teenager.

Don't tell children more than they want to know. They may have to think about what you said and may not understand it well enough to ask more questions until months later. Wait for questions. They will come in time. Do not be afraid that you told too much because the child will only think about the part that he or she feels is the answer to what he or she wants to know.

(continued...)

Level 7 Human Awareness

What should you do about four-letter words?

Children often use four-letter words to find out what they mean, or to see what adults will do. Do not be shocked at this, but try to teach the child at this time. Say the four-letter word back to him or her. This will show that you are not shocked or that saying the "dirty" word is not so great. Ask the child to tell you what the word means. Listen and then say what it means and how you feel about the way it was used. This is a time for you to tell him or her what your values are, how you think about things, or what is right or wrong.

If the child talks about things that make you think he or she may have been sexually abused, contact your pediatrician, clinic, or phone a child abuse hotline.

When the child asks questions that you don't have answers for, ask your family doctor, clinic, or health department.

REMEMBER:
If anything written here is against your religious or moral beliefs, don't do it!

❏ *Approval* ❏ *Acceptance* ❏ *Pride*
❏ *Self-respect* ❏ *Respect for Others*

● **EATING AND TALKING TOGETHER.**

1. Eat at least ONE MEAL a day together as a family (TV off).
2. Talk about what happened that day, how you felt and so on.
3. Have each one at the table tell ONE GOOD thing that happened that day. Be sure everyone gets a turn.
4. Praise everyone for sharing (telling the others their thoughts).
5. Have some rules. Everyone should try to share and not be afraid to tell their ideas and feelings. Do not tell someone that they are wrong. Do not "make fun" of something someone else is willing to share. Let someone tell everything they want before you say something. If you have nothing to say, you can PASS!

❏ *Sense of Power* ❏ *Responsibility*
❏ *Flexibility* ❏ *Pride*

● **LET THE CHILD PICK OUT HIS OR HER CLOTHES TO WEAR EACH DAY. THIS TEACHES THE CHILD TO MAKE A CHOICE AND LIVE WITH IT.**

1. You pick out two shirts or tops and pants.
2. Let the child pick out one of them to wear that day.
3. Talk about which colors may go together best.
4. Praise the child for his or her choice.
5. If the child changes his or her mind before putting it on, it is okay! After it is on, the child must live with the choice.
6. In front of the child, proudly tell the other parent, teacher, caseworker, visitor, "[Child's name] picked out his or her own shirt. He or she is getting so big."

❏ *Approval* ❏ *Acceptance*

● **TELL OR READ A STORY TO THE CHILD (about 5 minutes).**

1. You should do this about the same time every day when you can be with the child.
2. Let him or her pick out the book or story.
3. Sit next to the child.
4. Read the story the way the child likes it read. It is okay if he or she wants to skip pages or stop to talk about the story or pictures.
5. After the story, let the child tell you about what happened.
6. Praise him or her for being a good listener.
7. Say that you like doing this, and you plan to do it again.

❏ *Responsibility* ❏ *Self-respect*
❏ *Flexibility* ❏ *Pride*

● **THE CHILD LEARNS RESPONSIBILITY. GIVE HIM OR HER A TASK OR CHORE TO DO. AFTER IT IS FINISHED, GIVE THE CHILD SOMETHING (A REWARD) FOR DOING IT WELL.**

1. Talk with the child about everyone in the family having responsibility for helping around the house.
2. Pick out 3 things to do in the house that you think he or she can do well, simple things like empty the wastebasket, pick up toys.
3. Talk about how he or she is going to do these tasks or jobs. Help the child keep track of doing it every day for a week.
4. Make a calendar or check-off list for these tasks.
5. Tell the child that he or she will get a reward at the end of the week.
6. Keep doing the same task or chore each week until the child can do it well. Then the child can select a new task or chore.

❏ *Sense of Power* ❏ *Acceptance*
❏ *Flexibility* ❏ *Pride*

● **PLAY THE GAME "SIMON SAYS" TO HELP THE CHILD LEARN TO FOLLOW DIRECTIONS AND PLAY WITH OTHERS.**

1. Explain the game, "Simon Says." There are two kinds of directions: When "Simon Says" the direction, you do what "Simon Says" to do. If Simon doesn't say to do it—you don't do it.
2. Play the game. (Example)
"SIMON SAYS" take four giant steps backwards. (That's okay!)
"SIMON SAYS" wave your right hand. (That's okay!)
Take two steps forward. (Don't do it!)
"SIMON SAYS" clap your hands. (That's okay!)
Hop on one foot. (Don't do it!)
3. You can add your own things to do.
4. If the child does something SIMON did not say to do—they're out of the game. Have them go sit in a chair and count to 10—then they can become part of the game again.
5. Point out how well the child is listening and how important it is to follow instructions and listen carefully!

❏ *Approval* ❏ *Acceptance* ❏ *Sense of Power*
❏ *Responsibility* ❏ *Pride*

● *RESPONSIBILITY*—GIVE THE CHILD
A SPECIAL SPACE FOR HIS OR
HER THINGS.

1. Find a shelf, box or drawer that the child can get
   to easily.
2. Empty the space and turn it over to the child and
   say, "This is *your* space."
3. Help the child think about what things he or she
   has. The child should pick out what will be kept
   in the space.
4. Say "Those are good things for your space."
   Have the child put the things away. Tell the
   child what a good job he or she is doing, that it
   looks nice and neat.
5. If the child does not like this idea, forget it for
   now, but try again at a later time.
6. If he or she uses the space, tell the child to show
   it to others if he or she wants to—to Dad,
   Grandma, neighbor, etc. Be sure they know how
   well he or she takes care of it.
7. Check the space every day with the child. Praise
   the child for keeping the space together,
   straight, or neat. If it is not the way it should be,
   help him or her to get it "together".

❏ *Approval* ❏ *Acceptance*

● DANCING WITH A CHILD TO MUSIC IS
A GOOD ACTIVITY AND CAN BE FUN
(5 minutes).

1. Turn on the radio or phonograph.
2. Say, "Will you dance with me?"
3. Dance with child for one song.
4. Tell child: "I like to dance with you", or
   "This is fun!" (If you can't find music on
   the radio, sing.)

❏ *Trust*

● TALK WITH THE CHILD ABOUT
FAMILIES.

1. Meal time may be a good time to talk.
2. Things you want the child to know:
   A. Families may be made up in different ways.
      There may be only a father or a mother. A
      family may have grandparents, aunts, cousins,
      and so on. A family may be a stepfather or
      stepmother with children, so there are
      stepbrothers and stepsisters.
   B. No one kind of family is best. All kinds can
      be okay.
   C. Every family has different rules, and that's
      okay. No one set of rules is best or right.
      Everyone in the family must live by their
      family rules.
3. Ways to help the child when he or she says
   something about the different ones in the family.
   A. Everyone in the family can be different and
      have different things happen in their life.
      This is okay.
   B. You should not say that one child is better
      than the other in any way. They may be
      different, but don't let them get the feeling
      that he or she is better or not as good.

☐ *Approval* ☐ *Acceptance* ☐ *Pride*
☐ *Self-respect* ☐ *Respect for Others*

● **EATING AND TALKING TOGETHER.**

1. Eat at least ONE MEAL a day together as a family (TV off).
2. Talk about what happened that day, how you felt and so on.
3. Have each one at the table tell ONE GOOD thing that happened that day. Be sure everyone gets a turn.
4. Praise everyone for sharing (telling the others their thoughts).
5. Have some rules. Everyone should try to share and not be afraid to tell their ideas and feelings. Do not tell someone that they are wrong. Do not "make fun" of something someone else is willing to share. Let someone tell everything they want before you say something. If you have nothing to say, you can PASS!

☐ *Sense of Power* ☐ *Responsibility*
☐ *Flexibility* ☐ *Pride*

● **LET THE CHILD PICK OUT HIS OR HER CLOTHES TO WEAR EACH DAY. THIS TEACHES THE CHILD TO MAKE A CHOICE AND LIVE WITH IT.**

1. You pick out two shirts or tops and pants.
2. Let the child pick out one of them to wear that day.
3. Talk about which colors may go together best.
4. Praise the child for his or her choice.
5. If the child changes his or her mind before putting it on, it is okay! After it is on, the child must live with the choice.
6. In front of the child, proudly tell the other parent, teacher, caseworker, visitor, "[Child's name] picked out his or her own shirt. He or she is getting so big."

☐ *Approval* ☐ *Acceptance*

● **TELL OR READ A STORY TO THE CHILD (about 5 minutes).**

1. You should do this about the same time every day when you can be with the child.
2. Let him or her pick out the book or story.
3. Sit next to the child.
4. Read the story the way the child likes it read. It is okay if he or she wants to skip pages or stop to talk about the story or pictures.
5. After the story, let the child tell you about what happened.
6. Praise him or her for being a good listener.
7. Say that you like doing this, and you plan to do it again.

☐ *Approval* ☐ *Acceptance* ☐ *Sense of Power*
☐ *Responsibility* ☐ *Pride*

● *RESPONSIBILITY*—**GIVE THE CHILD A SPECIAL SPACE FOR HIS OR HER THINGS.**

1. Find a shelf, box or drawer that the child can get to easily.
2. Empty the space and turn it over to the child and say, "This is *your* space."
3. Help the child think about what things he or she has. The child should pick out what will be kept in the space.
4. Say "Those are good things for your space." Have the child put the things away. Tell the child what a good job he or she is doing, that it looks nice and neat.
5. If the child does not like this idea, forget it for now, but try again at a later time.
6. If he or she uses the space, tell the child to show it to others if he or she wants to—to Dad, Grandma, neighbor, etc. Be sure they know how well he or she takes care of it.
7. Check the space every day with the child. Praise the child for keeping the space together, straight, or neat. If it is not the way it should be, help him or her to get it "together".

☐ *Responsibility* ☐ *Self-respect*
☐ *Flexibility* ☐ *Pride*

● **THE CHILD LEARNS RESPONSIBILITY. GIVE HIM OR HER A TASK OR CHORE TO DO. AFTER IT IS FINISHED, GIVE THE CHILD SOMETHING (A REWARD) FOR DOING IT WELL.**

1. Talk with the child about everyone in the family having responsibility for helping around the house.
2. Pick out 3 things to do in the house that you think he or she can do well, simple things like empty the wastebasket, pick up toys.
3. Talk about how he or she is going to do these tasks or jobs. Help the child keep track of doing it every day for a week.
4. Make a calendar or check-off list for these tasks.
5. Tell the child that he or she will get a reward at the end of the week.
6. Keep doing the same task or chore each week until the child can do it well. Then the child can select a new task or chore.

Option for the family:
❏ *Sense of Power* ❏ *Acceptance*
❏ *Flexibility* ❏ *Pride*

● **PLAY THE GAME "SIMON SAYS" TO HELP THE CHILD LEARN TO FOLLOW DIRECTIONS AND PLAY WITH OTHERS.**

1. Explain the game, "Simon Says." There are two kinds of directions: When "Simon Says" the direction, you do what "Simon Says" to do. If Simon doesn't say to do it—you don't do it.

2. Play the game. (Example)
"SIMON SAYS" take four giant steps backwards. (That's okay!)
"SIMON SAYS" wave your right hand. (That's okay!)
Take two steps forward. (Don't do it!)
"SIMON SAYS"clap your hands. (That's okay!)
Hop on one foot. (Don't do it!)

3. You can add your own things to do.

4. If the child does something SIMON did not say to do—they're out of the game. Have them go sit in a chair and count to 10—then they can become part of the game again.

5. Point out how well the child is listening and how important it is to follow instructions and listen carefully!

❏ *Approval* ❏ *Acceptance*
● **IDENTIFYING DIFFERENT EMOTIONS.**
1. Get a magazine or picture book.
2. Select an emotion that you are going to search for together—happy, sad, anger, fear, etc.
3. Have some children tell you how they feel when they have the emotion.
4. Go through the book or magazine. Find pictures that show the selected emotion.
5. Have 4 children show the rest of the class how they look or act when they feel this emotion. They should try to look like the pictures. Tell them, "Say what you see in this picture." Don't ask, "How do you feel?"
6. If you see that the child looks unhappy, say "You look sad. Sometimes when I'm sad I need a big hug." Give a hug!, etc.

Option:
❏ *Sense of Power* ❏ *Acceptance*
❏ *Flexibility* ❏ *Pride*
● **PLAY THE GAME "SIMON SAYS" TO HELP THE CHILD LEARN TO FOLLOW DIRECTIONS AND PLAY WITH OTHERS.**
1. Explain the game, "Simon Says." There are two kinds of directions: When "Simon Says" the direction, you do what "Simon Says" to do. If Simon doesn't say to do it—you don't do it.
2. Play the game. (Example)
"SIMON SAYS" take four giant steps backwards. (That's okay!)
"SIMON SAYS" wave your right hand. (That's okay!)
Take two steps forward. (Don't do it!)
"SIMON SAYS" clap your hands. (That's okay!)
Hop on one foot. (Don't do it!)
3. You can add your own things to do.
4. If the child does something SIMON did not say to do—they're out of the game. Have them go sit in a chair and count to 10—then they can become part of the game again.
5. Point out how well the child is listening and how important it is to follow instructions and listen carefully!

PARENTS AS TEACHERS
USD 383
2031 POYNTZ AVE.
MANHATTAN, KS. 66502

❐ *Sense of Power* ❐ *Acceptance*
❐ *Flexibility* ❐ *Pride*

● **PLAY THE GAME "SIMON SAYS" TO HELP THE CHILD LEARN TO FOLLOW DIRECTIONS AND PLAY WITH OTHERS.**

1. Explain the game, "Simon Says." There are two kinds of directions: When "Simon Says" the direction, you do what "Simon Says" to do. If Simon doesn't say to do it—you don't do it.
2. Play the game. (Example)
"SIMON SAYS" take four giant steps backwards. (That's okay!)
"SIMON SAYS" wave your right hand. (That's okay!)
Take two steps forward. (Don't do it!)
"SIMON SAYS" clap your hands. (That's okay!)
Hop on one foot. (Don't do it!)
3. You can add your own things to do.
4. If the child does something SIMON did not say to do—they're out of the game. Have them go sit in a chair and count to 10—then they can become part of the game again.
5. Point out how well the child is listening and how important it is to follow instructions and listen carefully!

❐ *Approval* ❐ *Acceptance*

● **DANCING WITH A CHILD TO MUSIC IS A GOOD ACTIVITY AND CAN BE FUN (5 minutes).**

1. Turn on the radio or phonograph.
2. Say, "Will you dance with me?"
3. Dance with child for one song.
4. Tell child: "I like to dance with you", or "This is fun!" (If you can't find music on the radio, sing.)

❐ *Approval* ❐ *Acceptance*

● **SHARING FEELINGS OR WORRIES.**

1. If in office or home, provide child a piece of paper with 2 or 3 crayons.
2. Suggest he or she draw a picture of one of the following (selecting 1 emotion per visit): HAPPY, MAD, SCARY, SAD.
3. Ask him or her to tell about the picture.
4. PRAISE placement of objects in the picture, use of colors, etc.
5. If your visit with the child is on the move, suggest a "Story Starter" to the child with one of the above feelings. Ask the child to make up a story or tell a REAL one he or she may know. If it's made up, you can add a sentence here and there to keep the story moving.
6. Pick out the POSITIVE things being said to discuss further and reinforce with the child.
7. Make sure that the conversation ends on a POSITIVE note. This keeps you in a favorable light until you have the opportunity to meet again.

Level 8 Characteristics

- Curious
- Knows primary colors
- Plays well with same sex
- Skips
- More cooperative
- Plays in groups
- Sensitive to ridicule (feeling hurt easily)
- Likes to be around adults (mimics their behavior)
- Is into the "right" way
- Shares family gossip
- Sociable
- Silly
- Likes to make things
- Able to make up own stories or songs
- Speaks in complete sentences
- Has hand coordination
- Draws figures
- Likes physical activity
- Able to follow 2- and 3-step directions
- Knows difference between the truth and a lie
- Likes to look nice

Level 8 Information

Self-esteem is a feeling.
If you have HIGH self-esteem...
  You make good friends!
  You care about yourself and other people;
  You are responsible;
  You enjoy learning;
  You are proud of what you do;
  You can handle failure;
  You can share feelings.

HIGH self-esteem is having a GOOD feeling about yourself, your place in the family, your school, and your world.

THINGS TO REMEMBER:
  • When you first see the child after school or work and the child has done something wrong and you are upset, try to say at least 2 GOOD THINGS to him or her BEFORE you talk about any bad things.
  • If the child cannot do the activity right...it's okay and the child is okay!
  • KEEP TRYING!
  • LOOK for the Good Stuff!
  • When he or she does something GOOD, tell him or her.
  • When the child SHARES...PRAISE!
  • Children take things in their life VERY SERIOUSLY. You should, too. This shows RESPECT for the child.
  • Whisper something "special" and "nice" to the child.
  • A pat on the shoulder or a big hug shows you care.
  • Keep adult sexual activity private.
  • Same bed time and bath time EVERY night.
  • Do not walk around the house nude.
  • Do not use foul language around the child.
  • FIND A REASON TO SAY EACH OF THESE PHRASES ONCE A DAY!
    That's really nice!
    I like the way you did it.

DON'T GIVE UP!
— If the child does not want to do the activity with you the way you want him or her to...try again tomorrow.
— Keep trying. This is the way you **SHOW** the child that you mean what you say. A child needs to **TRUST** in order to share with you or listen to you.
— **HOW** you say something is sometimes more important than **WHAT** you say.

You may be doing MOST of these things already as part of the way you care for children and run your home. By doing these things in the way they are written, you will be helping the child's self-esteem **plus** your own self-esteem.

When you can help somebody feel good... you feel good!

"I" messages let the child know exactly what you want, why you want it, and how you want it. The child does not have to GUESS what you want or how you feel. This is a way of setting LIMITS. Some examples are:
  • "**I** feel very upset when you throw your clothes on the floor. Clothes cost money... **I** work hard for my money and **I** want you to have nice clothes to wear."
  • "**I** do not want you to carry those two full glasses of milk at one time. **I** am afraid they will spill."

The BASE program is about helping children have HIGH self-esteem. It is a group of things to do and share with a child. These things are short, simple and positive. They should be done everyday when possible.

REMEMBER:
If any of these things do not agree with the way you believe or your religion (example: dancing), do not do it.

Level 8 Human Awareness

Here are some things for you to talk about with your child. It means a lot for you to let the child know that you want to talk about these things.

BOTH PARENTS SHOULD PARTICIPATE. When possible, both parents should share the responsibility for sex education. Men have expected most sex education to be done by the mother. When both parents participate, the child sees sex education as a family affair.

How to get the child to ask questions:

Listen to what he or she talks about and when the time is right tell him or her some things. The child may tell you about how many puppies the dog next door had. Then you may say, "Yes, dogs have more children at a time than people do. We have one or two babies at a time." This gives him or her a chance to ask more questions.

What you should say when the child asks you something:

Always answer. Do not wait to tell what he or she wants to know, even if it seems that he or she is asking in order to shock you. Do not say, "I'll tell you when you are older". Answer in the right way and with good information for the child's age. You build self-esteem when you answer. If you *do not* tell what he or she wants to know, the child learns: 1. not to ask you things; or, 2. that he or she is not "big" enough or "good" enough.

The genitals are sometimes called the "private parts" of the body. In a child, they are at the bottom of the body. Use the right names when you talk about the genitals.

If the child is touching his or her private parts when with other people or out of the house you should:

1. Try to get him or her to think about something else by talking to him or her, showing him or her something, and so on;
2. Do not try to do something about it right then. Do not make a big deal about it. Do not put the child down.
3. Later, when you are at home with him or her and no one is with you, say "It's okay to touch yourself there, but that is something we do not do when others are around."

If he or she asks you where a baby comes from, say: "There is a special place between Mommy's legs that the baby comes out of".

What should you do about four-letter words?

Children often use four-letter words to find out what they mean, or to see what adults will do. Do not be shocked at this, but try to teach the child at this time. Say the four-letter word back to him or her. This will show that you are not shocked or that saying the "dirty" word is not so great. Ask the child to tell you what the word means. Listen and then say what it means and how you feel about the way it was used. This is a time for you to tell him or her what your values are, how you think about things, or what is right or wrong.

Telling children about sex will not make them think more about it. It will not lead them to experimenting or trying to do it.

(continued...)

Level 8 Human Awareness

Talk about people. When a child wants to know about the body or how babies are made, he or she is thinking about people. When you answer the questions by talking about cats and dogs, the child will not think that it is the same in people.

Children want short answers that are to the point.

Don't be afraid to say, "I don't know". You should then try to find the answer. There are books about this that the child can understand. First read the book by yourself so that you know what is in it. Then read it *with* the child.

Be sure you know what your own values are…how you think about things…what is right or wrong.

It is okay to talk together about different ways of thinking; ways that may be different from the way you may feel.

Let the child know that you want to be asked questions and will answer them. Don't say, "I'll tell you when you're older." Try to teach when things happen (like on TV, or radio, in newspapers, or magazines), with your friends, other children, or someone in the family.

Let the child know that it is normal and okay for there to be changes in his or her body.

Keep your sense of humor.

Don't try to be perfect. No one is always right.

If the child talks about things that make you think he or she may have been sexually abused, contact your pediatrician, clinic, or phone a child abuse hotline.

When the child asks questions that you don't have answers for, ask your family doctor, clinic, or health department.

REMEMBER:
If anything written here is against your religious or moral beliefs, don't do it!

Level 8 Teacher Information

(To be used with **C** Exercises)

Your cooperation with these exercises is VERY IMPORTANT.

As you know, success or failure in school is directly tied to self-esteem. The intelligent child with low self-esteem will do poorly in school...the average child with HIGH self-esteem will generally be successful.

It's also true that low self-esteem gets in the way of good performance and that bad performance reinforces low self-esteem.

This exercise can be done with the child alone in the beginning. Within a week or so, you might want to share it with the entire class. This exercise works very well as a "calmer downer" after recess, or break.

This is a way of trying to show a little **extra special attention** to a child who is very much in need of POSITIVE strokes.

Look for the POSITIVE and PRAISE it. Use the child's name when giving PRAISE. Be specific with the PRAISE.

Your support is appreciated!

❏ *Approval* ❏ *Acceptance* ❏ *Pride*

● **PRAISE THE CHILD FOR THINGS HE OR SHE DOES.**

1. Look at any art work the child does or brings home from school.
2. Put pictures on refrigerator. Take them down after a week and put up new pictures. You can keep some in a special box or folder.
3. Have the family look at the pictures.
4. Try to have him or her sing songs or tell a story heard at school.
5. Praise the work. Do not tell the child ways to make it better or that someone's work is better than his or hers.

❏ *Approval* ❏ *Acceptance* ❏ *Trust*
❏ *Self-respect* ❏ *Respect for Others*

● **TELL EACH OTHER ONE THING YOU LIKED ABOUT "YOURSELF" THAT DAY.**

1. Pick a time when you and the child are not in a hurry to do something else.
2. Pick a place where there is no one with you and the child.
3. Tell the child that you liked the way he or she did something today. Do not talk about how he or she looked.
4. Ask the child to tell you something good that he or she did today.
5. If the child does not want to do this, you can tell him or her something you saw: "You played with your friend in a nice way" or "You put your toys away."

❏ *Acceptance* ❏ *Responsibility* ❏ *Pride*

● **THE PARENT AND CHILD SHOULD WORK IN THE SAME ROOM, BUT EACH DO HIS OR HER OWN JOB.**

1. The parent picks two jobs to be done in the same room. The parent may dust while the child picks up toys.
2. Talk to each other while working.
3. Tell the child that he or she is doing something good: "I like your help", "You are putting those things away the right way."
4. If the child does a good job, be sure to say so and thank him or her. If it was not a good job, try to tell something that was done well, like "You tried hard" or "You put some things away." *You may then want to tell the child some things that can be done the next time to make it a better job.* (Do not do the work over when he or she is there if you don't like the way the work was done.)
5. In this way, the child learns how to get the job

done...done the best way it can be done...done the way you want it done. It's very important to work together in this way!

❏ *Acceptance* ❏ *Respect for Others*

● **DO SOME ACTIVITIES TOGETHER.**

1. Plan a "family night" when you all do something together.
2. Let the children plan what you will eat tonight. They should pick things that are okay with you.
3. Watch TV together, or play a game, or read a story or comic together.

❏ *Trust*

● **TALK WITH THE CHILD ABOUT FAMILIES.**

1. Meal time may be a good time to talk.
2. Things you want the child to know:
   A. Families may be made up in different ways. There may be only a father or mother. A family may have grandparents, aunts, cousins, and so on. A family may be a stepfather or stepmother with children, so there are stepbrothers and stepsisters.
   B. No one kind of family is best. All kinds can be okay.
   C. Every family has different rules, and that's okay. No set of rules is best or right. Everyone in the family must live by their own family rules.
3. Ways to help the child when he or she says something about the different ones in the family:
   A. Everyone in the family can be different and have different things happen in their life. This is okay.
   B. You should not say that one child is better than the other in any way. They may be different, but don't let them get the feeling that he or she is better, or not as good.

❏ *Approval* ❏ *Acceptance*

● **READ A STORY TO THE CHILD OR LOOK AT MAGAZINES TOGETHER.**

1. Read a story or book if the child likes it.
2. Let him or her pick one magazine from two that you show the child.
3. Let the child make up a story from the pictures he or she sees.
4. Talk about the story you read or the pictures you looked at.
5. Praise the child for doing this with you.

❏ *Approval* ❏ *Pride* ❏ *Acceptance*
❏ *Self-respect* ❏ *Respect for Others*

● WHEN EATING, EACH ONE IN THE FAMILY CAN TELL A GOOD THING THAT HAPPENED TO THEM TODAY.

1. Do this each day when most of the family is eating together.
2. You say, "Who wants to be the first to tell us some **good things** that happened today?"
3. Try to pick someone different each day to start.
4. Praise the child for telling you this and for sharing.
5. Give each a turn to tell something if he or she wants to.
6. If someone does not want to share—they can "PASS".
7. You share something, too.
8. Some good things to talk about are:
   (1) something nice you saw; (2) something you did for somebody; or (3) something nice you heard or any other nice things.

❏ *Approval* ❏ *Trust* ❏ *Acceptance*

● ASK THE CHILD ABOUT HIS OR HER DAY.

1. Find a quiet time at the end of school, or later in the day when the two of you are alone.
2. Ask the child about his or her day. "What did you do in school?", "What was fun?", "Tell me about one thing you learned today.", "Did you hear a story?"
3. If the child tells you about something that was not nice, talk about it. ("Did it make you sad when that happened?")
4. In this way you tell the child that the things he or she does during the day are important—and that you care!

❏ *Approval* ❏ *Acceptance*

● ASK THE CHILD TO DRAW A PICTURE OF SOMETHING GOOD THAT HAPPENED TO HIM OR HER TODAY.

1. Pick a time when you and the child are not doing something else and not in a hurry.
2. Get some crayons and paper.
3. Ask the child to draw something he or she liked that day or some good thing he or she did.
4. Have the child tell you about the picture.
5. Pick out something in the picture (a color or thing) you really like and tell that you like it and why.

❏ *Sense of Power* ❏ *Responsibility* ❏ *Pride*

● PICK ONE OR TWO JOBS THE CHILD CAN DO.

1. Pick things like setting the table or taking out trash. (If the child is small…picking up toys or making the bed.)
2. You show the child how to do the job. If he or she sets the table, draw a picture on a card to show where to put things (napkin, fork, plate, knife, spoon).
3. Praise the child for doing the job. (Do not do it over if it is not done right.)
4. Make a chart for a week. Put a mark on each day the job was done *right*. You may want to give the child something special after doing a good job for a week. Example:

	S	M	T	W	TH	F	S
Put toys away	x	x					
Make bed		x	x				

❏ *Approval* ❏ *Responsibility* ❏ *Pride*

● THE CHILD SHOULD PUT AWAY HIS OR HER OWN TOYS.

1. Tell the child to stop playing and start putting the things away. Praise him or her for doing this. "Good, you know what to do."
2. Tell the child some things to do. "Put the blocks in this bag." "Put the doll and her things in your room."
3. If he or she helps put things away, be sure to praise him or her for the work.
4. Praise the child for being "responsible" when all the things are put away.
5. If the child will not help, take him or her to do some other thing that you may need help doing and ask the child to help you.

❏ *Approval* ❏ *Pride* ❏ *Acceptance*
❏ *Self-respect* ❏ *Respect for Others*

● **WHEN EATING, EACH ONE IN THE FAMILY CAN TELL A GOOD THING THAT HAPPENED TO THEM TODAY.**

1. Do this each day when most of the family is eating together.
2. You say, "Who wants to be the first to tell us some **good things** that happened today?"
3. Try to pick someone different each day to start.
4. Praise the child for telling you this and for sharing.
5. Give each a turn to tell something if he or she wants to.
6. If someone does not want to share—they can "PASS".
7. You share something, too.
8. Some good things to talk about are: (1) something nice you saw; (2) something you did for somebody; or (3) something nice you heard or any other nice things.

❏ *Approval* ❏ *Trust* ❏ *Acceptance*

● **ASK THE CHILD ABOUT HIS OR HER DAY.**

1. Find a quiet time at the end of school, or later in the day when the two of you are alone.
2. Ask the child about his or her day. "What did you do in school?", "What was fun?", "Tell me about one thing you learned today.", "Did you hear a story?"
3. If the child tells you about something that was not nice, talk about it. ("Did it make you sad when that happened?")
4. In this way you tell the child that the things he or she does during the day are important—and that you care!

❏ *Approval* ❏ *Acceptance*

● **ASK THE CHILD TO DRAW A PICTURE OF SOMETHING GOOD THAT HAPPENED TO HIM OR HER TODAY.**

1. Pick a time when you and the child are not doing something else and not in a hurry.
2. Get some crayons and paper.
3. Ask the child to draw something he or she liked that day or some good thing he or she did.
4. Have the child tell you about the picture.
5. Pick out something in the picture (a color or thing) you really like and tell that you like it and why.

❏ *Sense of Power* ❏ *Responsibility* ❏ *Pride*

● **PICK ONE OR TWO JOBS THE CHILD CAN DO.**

1. Pick things like setting the table or taking out trash. (If the child is small…picking up toys or making the bed.)
2. You show the child how to do the job. If he or she sets the table, draw a picture on a card to show where to put things (napkin, fork, plate, knife, spoon).
3. Praise the child for doing the job. (Do not do it over if it is not done right.)
4. Make a chart for a week. Put a mark on each day the job was done *right*. You may want to give the child something special after doing a good job for a week. Example:

	S	M	T	W	TH	F	S
Put toys away	x	x					
Make bed		x	x				

❏ *Approval* ❏ *Responsibility* ❏ *Pride*

● **THE CHILD SHOULD PUT AWAY HIS OR HER OWN TOYS.**

1. Tell the child to stop playing and start putting the things away. Praise him or her for doing this. "Good, you know what to do."
2. Tell the child some things to do. "Put the blocks in this bag." "Put the doll and her things in your room."
3. If he or she helps put things away, be sure to praise him or her for the work.
4. Praise the child for being "responsible" when all the things are put away.
5. If the child will not help, take him or her to do some other thing that you may need help doing and ask the child to help you.

❏ *Approval* ❏ *Acceptance* ❏ *Pride*

● **PRAISE THE CHILD FOR THINGS HE OR SHE DOES.**

1. Look at any art work the child does or brings home from school.
2. Put pictures on refrigerator. Take them down after a week and put up new pictures. You can keep some in a special box or folder.
3. Have the family look at the pictures.
4. Try to have him or her sing songs or tell a story heard at school.
5. Praise the work. Do not tell the child ways to make it better or that someone's work is better than his or hers.

❏ *Approval* ❏ *Acceptance* ❏ *Trust*
❏ *Self-respect* ❏ *Respect for Others*

● **TELL EACH OTHER ONE THING YOU LIKED ABOUT "YOURSELF" THAT DAY.**

1. Pick a time when you and the child are not in a hurry to do something else.
2. Pick a place where there is no one with you and the child.
3. Tell the child that you liked the way he or she did something today. Do not talk about how he or she looked.
4. Ask the child to tell you something good that he or she did today.
5. If the child does not want to do this, you can tell him or her something you saw: "You played with your friend in a nice way", or "You put your toys away."

❏ *Acceptance* ❏ *Responsibility* ❏ *Pride*

● **THE PARENT AND CHILD SHOULD WORK IN THE SAME ROOM, BUT EACH DO HIS OR HER OWN JOB.**

1. The parent picks two jobs to be done in the same room. The parent may dust while the child picks up toys.
2. Talk to each other while working.
3. Tell the child that he or she is doing something good: "I like your help", "You are putting those things away the right way."
4. If the child does a good job, be sure to say so and thank him or her. If it was not a good job, try to tell something that was done well, like "You tried hard", or "You put some things away." *You may then want to tell the child some things that can be done the next time to make it a better job.* (Do not do the work over when he or she is there if you don't like the way the work was done.)
5. In this way, the child learns how to get the job done...done the best way it can be done...done the way you want it done. It's very important to work together in this way!

❏ *Acceptance* ❏ *Respect for Others*

● **DO SOME ACTIVITIES TOGETHER.**

1. Plan a "family night" when you all do something together.
2. Let the children plan what you will eat tonight. They should pick things that are okay with you.
3. Watch TV together, or play a game, or read a story or comic together.

READ CAREFULLY BEFORE YOU DO THIS EXERCISE WITH THE CHILD OR CLASS.

❏ *Trust*

● **RELAXATION (Getting in touch with yourself—taking control of YOU!)**
(Suggestion: This is a great exercise for the entire class after recess. It can be a relaxer for everyone!)

1. Close your eyes or look down into your lap.
2. Sit straight in your chair. Feet flat on the floor.
3. Let your arms and hands hang loose at your sides.
4. Now, start at your toes: tighten the muscles in your foot—tight—tight (feel the muscles).
5. Have the tight, tight muscles move up your legs—all the way up—above your chest—out your arms—to your hands—make a FIST tight, tighter.
6. Make your whole body tight.
7. Now, we're going to begin to relax.
8. Starting with your toes. Relax. Feel your toes wiggle.
9. Relax. Relax. Feel the muscles.
10. Relax your fists—let your hands hang loose.
11. Sit quietly—Keep your eyes closed. Relax. Relax! (Sit still for 10 seconds.)

OPTIONS:

❏ *Acceptance* ❏ *Pride*

1. Find out about a chore or task child does at home.
2. Find out child's interest, find something he or she is interested in. Direct child to a related book or magazine on the subject. Continue to show your interest in the child's interest choice.
3. Praise child for neat locker or space that is his or hers in the classroom.

❏ *Acceptance*

● **DO SOMETHING WITH THE CHILD THAT IS FUN FOR BOTH OF YOU. OTHERS CAN BE WITH YOU.**

1. Pick something you all like to do:
   Take a walk.
   Skip together.
   Play a game like "Simon Says" or "Hopscotch", or others.
   Pick up leaves or other things from the ground, lawn, park, or fields.
2. Talk with the child.
3. Praise the child for seeing or doing things.

❏ *Approval* ❏ *Acceptance*

● **READ A STORY TO THE CHILD OR LOOK AT MAGAZINES TOGETHER.**

1. Read a story or book if the child likes it.
2. Let him or her pick one magazine from two that you show the child.
3. Let the child make up a story from the pictures he or she sees.
4. Talk about the story you read or the pictures you looked at.
5. Praise the child for doing this with you.

❏ *Acceptance* ❏ *Pride*

● **TALK WITH THE CHILD FOR A MINUTE OR SO. FIND OUT WHAT HE OR SHE LIKES TO DO, SUCH AS SPORTS, COLLECTING THINGS, PLAYING GAMES, ETC.**

1. Pick a quiet time to talk when you are away from others.
2. Ask the child about the things he or she likes to do. Try to get the child to tell you more by asking things.
3. Ask what he or she wants to do that he or she is not doing now.
4. Let the child know that you like to hear about the things he or she does.
5. Talk to the child about some other things he or she can do. If the child likes to play ball, he or she can throw it, catch it, kick a big ball like playing soccer, etc.
6. Praise the child for what he or she does.
7. Try to have something with you the next time you talk that will be about the thing he or she likes to do. It may be a book from the library, a picture, a magazine, etc.

❏ *Approval* ❏ *Trust* ❏ *Acceptance*

● **ASK THE CHILD ABOUT HIS OR HER DAY.**

1. Find a quiet time at the end of school, or later in the day when the two of you are alone.
2. Ask the child about his or her day. "What did you do in school?", "What was fun?", "Tell me about one thing you learned today.", "Did you hear a story?"
3. If the child tells you about something that was not nice, talk about it. ("Did it make you sad when that happened?")
4. In this way you tell the child that the things he or she does during the day are important—and that you care!

❏ *Approval* ❏ *Acceptance* ❏ *Trust* ❏ *Self-respect* ❏ *Respect for Others*

● **TELL EACH OTHER ONE THING YOU LIKED ABOUT "YOURSELF" THAT DAY.**

1. Pick a time when you and the child are not in a hurry to do something else.
2. Pick a place where there is no one with you and the child.
3. Tell the child that you liked the way he or she did something today. Do not talk about how he or she looked.
4. Ask the child to tell you something good that he or she did today.
5. If the child does not want to do this, you can tell him or her something you saw: "You played with your friend in a nice way", or "You put your toys away."

1st-2nd grade

Level 9 Characteristics

- Active, constant movement; shoving, talking, wiggling
- Imitates/role plays
- Begins activity in organized groups (Boy Scouts, etc.)
- Developing an understanding of consequences of behavior
- Verbally outspoken ("You stink", a know-it-all, tattle tale)
- Likes to make things
- May like to be center of attention
- Free with opinions and advice
- Affectionate
- Competitive with siblings
- Will pair with best friend
- Positive attitude and pride toward school
- Has likes and dislikes (food, activities, people, etc.)
- Increased sense of self and reactions of others
- Sensitive to disapproval or criticism
- Wants to be liked
- Helpful around house
- Likes solitary activities
- Considerate of adults
- Needs teacher approval and guidance
- Needs and wants structure
- Changing behaviors and moods
- Takes directions well

Level 9 Information

Self-esteem is a feeling.
If you have HIGH self-esteem...
  You make good friends!
  You care about yourself and other people;
  You are responsible;
  You enjoy learning;
  You are proud of what you do;
  You can handle failure;
  You can share feelings.

HIGH self-esteem is having a GOOD feeling about yourself, your place in the family, your school, and your world.

THINGS TO REMEMBER:
  • Same bath time and bed time EVERY night.
  • Do not walk around the house nude.
  • Do not use foul language in front of the child.
  • When you first see the child after work or school and the child has done something wrong and you are upset, try to say at least 2 GOOD THINGS to him or her BEFORE you talk about any bad things.
  • Use the child's name.
  • PRAISE for SHARING!
  • Keep adult sexual activity private.
  • FIND A REASON TO SAY EACH OF THESE PHRASES ONCE A DAY:
    Good thinking!
    You did that very well!

DON'T GIVE UP!
— If the child does not want to do the activity with you the way you want him or her to...try again tomorrow.
— Keep trying. This is the way you **SHOW** the child that you mean what you say. A child needs to **TRUST** in order to share with you or listen to you.
— **HOW** you say something is sometimes more important than **WHAT** you say.

You may be doing MOST of these things already as part of the way you care for children and run your home. By doing these things in the way they are written, you will be helping the child's self-esteem **plus** your own self-esteem.

When you can help somebody feel good... you feel good!

"I" messages let the child know exactly what you want, why you want it, and how you want it. The child does not have to GUESS what you want or how you feel. This is a way of setting LIMITS. Some examples are:
  • "I feel very upset when you throw your clothes on the floor. Clothes cost money... **I** work hard for my money and **I** want you to have nice clothes to wear."
  • "I do not want you to carry those two full glasses of milk at one time. **I** am afraid they will spill."

The BASE program is about helping children have HIGH self-esteem. It is a group of things to do and share with a child. These things are short, simple and positive. They should be done everyday when possible.

REMEMBER:
If any of these things do not agree with the way you believe or your religion (example: dancing), do not do it.

Level 9 Human Awareness

Here are some things for you to talk about with your child. It means a lot for you to let the child know that you want to talk about these things.

BOTH PARENTS SHOULD PARTICIPATE. When possible, both parents should share the responsibility for sex education. Men have expected most sex education to be done by the mother. When both parents participate, the child sees sex education as a family affair.

What you should say when the child asks you something:

Always answer. Do not wait to tell what he or she wants to know, even if it seems that he or she is asking in order to shock you. Do not say, "I'll tell you when you are older". Answer in the right way and with good information for the child's age. You build self-esteem when you answer. If you do not tell what he or she wants to know, the child learns: 1. not to ask you things; or, 2. that he or she is not "big" enough or "good" enough; or, 3. that you do not think the questions are important.

What should you do about four-letter words?

Children often use four-letter words to find out what they mean, or to see what adults will do. Do not be shocked at this, but try to teach the child at this time. Say the four-letter word back to him or her. This will show that you are not shocked or that saying the "dirty" word is not so great. Ask the child to tell you what the word means. Listen and then say what it means and how you feel about the way it was used. This is a time for you to tell him or her what your values are, how you think about things, or what is right or wrong.

Telling children about sex will not make them think more about it. It will not lead them to experimenting or trying to do it.

Talk about people. When a child wants to know about the body or how babies are made, he or she is thinking about people. When you answer the questions by talking about cats and dogs, the child will not think that it is the same in people.

Children want short answers that are to the point.

Don't be afraid to say, "I don't know". You should then try to find the answer. There are books about this that the child can understand. First read the book by yourself so that you know what is in it. Then read it *with* the child.

Be sure you know what your own values are...how you think about things...what is right or wrong.

It is okay to talk together about different ways of thinking; ways that may be different from the way you may feel.

Let the child know that you want to be asked questions and will answer them. Don't say, "I'll tell you when you're older." Try to teach when things happen (like on TV, or radio, in newspapers, or magazines), with your friends, other children, or someone in the family.

Let the child know that it is normal and okay for there to be changes in his or her body.

Keep your sense of humor.

(continued...)

Level 9 Human Awareness

Don't try to be perfect. No one is always right.

Some children do not ask questions. This does not mean the child doesn't have any questions. He or she may think about many things and have the wrong idea or wrong information about what he or she is thinking about.

DON'T WAIT FOR THE CHILD TO ASK! If he or she isn't asking questions about sex, it may be because the child got the feeling from you that you don't talk about sex in your home. It is your job to see that he or she knows the right things about sex, and does not have wrong information.

When you talk about sex, don't talk to the boys alone or girls alone. Boys and girls need to know how the other's body works. Boys will be living around women all their lives. They need to know about ovulation, contraception (how to keep from getting pregnant or sexual diseases), and menstruation (the period or "curse"). Girls also need to know how the man's body works. You want to be sure they learn that sex is something that the family can talk about.

When you talk about something that is hard for you, it is okay to say, "This makes me uncomfortable, but because I love you, it's something we need to talk about." The child might be just as uncomfortable or as embarrassed as you are!

If the child talks about things that make you think he or she may have been sexually abused, contact your pediatrician, clinic, or phone a child abuse hotline.

When the child asks questions that you don't have answers for, ask your family doctor, clinic, or health department.

REMEMBER:
If anything written here is against your religious or moral beliefs, don't do it!

Level 9 Teacher Information

(To be used with **C** Exercises)

Your cooperation with these exercises is VERY IMPORTANT.

As you know, success or failure in school is directly tied to self-esteem. The intelligent child with low self-esteem will do poorly in school...the average child with HIGH self-esteem will generally be successful.

It's also true that low self-esteem gets in the way of good performance and that bad performance reinforces low self-esteem.

This exercise can be done with the child alone in the beginning. Within a week or so, you might want to share it with the entire class. This exercise works very well as a "calmer downer" after recess, or break.

This is a way of trying to show a little **extra special attention** to a child who is very much in need of POSITIVE strokes.

**Look for the POSITIVE and PRAISE it.
Use the child's name when giving PRAISE.
Be specific with the PRAISE.**

Your support is appreciated!

❏ *Sense of Importance*

● **TRY TO FIND OUT THE THINGS THE CHILD LIKES TO DO OR WHAT HE OR SHE WANTS TO LEARN ABOUT. (THIS IS SOMETHING THE CHILD IS INTERESTED IN.)**

1. Talk with the child about his or her interest. An interest may last only one week and then he or she may have a new interest. This is okay.
2. If the child does not have an interest, try to help him or her find one. His or her interest may be animals, cars, trains, airplanes, plants, sports, and so on.
3. Some things you can do to help the child with his or her interest:
   Go to the library with him or her for books.
   Find magazine or newspaper articles.
   Read the article to the child.
   Go to places like the zoo, museum, nature center, and so on.

❏ *Pride* ❏ *Sense of Importance*

● **LET THE CHILD MAKE AND BRING SOMETHING TO HIS OR HER MOM, DAD, OTHER RELATIVE, OR FRIEND.**

1. Pick a time for the child to draw a picture, make something like a card, or something that he or she can bring on the next visit.
2. Give the child paper, crayon, pencil, and so on.
3. Praise the child for doing something for someone.

❏ *Pride* ❏ *Sense of Importance*

● **ASK THE CHILD TO HELP YOU READ A STORY.**

1. Ask if the child wants to help you read to a doll, pet, pretend friend, someone older, or a young child.
2. Let him or her pick out the book to read.
3. Start to read. He or she can talk about the story or pictures as you read, or may read some words with you.
4. Praise the child for the help.
5. He or she may not want to read a book but may be happy to tell a story he or she heard (maybe from school). Praise the child for doing this.
6. Keep doing this. The child will learn to like to read.

❏ *Acceptance* ❏ *Respect for Others*

● **WATCH AN "EDUCATIONAL" TV SHOW WITH THE CHILD.**

1. Pick out the TV show.
2. Let everyone in the family know about the show. Try to have most of them watch it with you.
3. Try not to do anything else while the TV show is on.
4. When the show is over, talk about what you saw with the child. Be sure he or she tells what he or she liked or didn't like about it. Do this for two or three minutes.
5. Thank the child for telling you his or her feelings. Anything he or she feels is okay.

❏ *Sense of Power* ❏ *Pride*
❏ *Sense of Importance*

● **YOU AND THE CHILD SHOULD DO SOMETHING OUTSIDE ONE OR TWO TIMES A WEEK.**

1. Some things you could do: picnic on the porch or in the park, watch the child skateboard, push him or her on a swing, take a walk, play in the yard or playground.
2. Let the child make the plans and tell you what to do.
3. Let the child know that you like doing these things.

❏ *Trust*

● **TALK WITH THE CHILD ABOUT FAMILIES.**

1. Meal time may be a good time to talk.
2. Things you want the child to know:
   A. Families may be made up in different ways. There may be only a father or mother. A family may have grandparents, aunts, cousins, and so on. A family may be a stepfather or stepmother with children, so there are stepbrothers and stepsisters.
   B. No one kind of family is best. All kinds can be okay.
   C. Every family has different rules, and that's okay. No set of rules is best or right. Everyone in the family must live by their own family rules.
3. Ways to help the child when he or she says something about the different ones in the family:
   A. Everyone in the family can be different and have different things happen in their life. This is okay.

(continued...)

B. You should not say that one child is better than the other in any way. They may be different, but don't let them get the feeling that he or she is better, or not as good.

❏ *Responsibility* ❏ *Self-respect* ❏ *Pride*
- **HELP THE CHILD LEARN TO BRUSH HIS OR HER TEETH, COMB HIS OR HER HAIR, AND DRESS BEFORE GOING TO SCHOOL.**
1. The child should learn one of these at a time. When it can be done without help, work on the next thing.
2. Get the child up early enough in the morning so there is time to do these things and not rush.
3. Have the toothbrush, toothpaste, hairbrush, comb, and clothes for school where the child can get them.
4. Tell the child that he or she is big and can brush his or her teeth. Help and watch him or her do this. When the child is good at it, tell him or her it is his or her job to do it every day.
5. Praise the child for doing this on his or her own. Let the family praise him or her.
6. Go on to the next thing—taking care of his or her hair, or putting on clothes.

❏ *Sense of Power* ❏ *Responsibility*
❏ *Pride* ❏ *Sense of Importance*
- **HELP THE CHILD PICK OUT HIS OR HER CLOTHES.**
1. Show the child which clothes look nice together. Show which colors go well together. Praise when the child does this.
2. Tell the child "You want to look nice. It makes you feel good when you do and when your friends like the way you look."
3. Praise him or her by saying, "You did a nice job dressing today.", "I like the way you combed your hair.", "That shirt and pants look nice together."

❏ *Sense of Power* ❏ *Responsibility*
❏ *Pride* ❏ *Sense of Importance*
- **THE CHILD LEARNS TO HANG UP HIS OR HER COAT AND PUT SCHOOL PAPERS AND BOOKS WHERE THEY SHOULD BE.**
1. Tell the child, "You are bigger and can do some things by yourself."
2. Show where to put the coat, papers and books. Tell the child that you like to see his or her work.
3. Help the child do this every day after school.
4. Let the child show you some papers. Talk about the work. Do this about the same time each day.
5. When he or she hangs up the coat and puts school work away with no help, praise the child.

❏ *Acceptance* ❏ *Responsibility* ❏ *Pride*
- **TALK WITH THE CHILD ABOUT HIS OR HER SCHOOL PAPERS EACH DAY.**
1. Let the child know that you like to hear about the school work and see the papers.
2. Talk about the work. Tell what you think is good about the work. Praise the work that is right.
3. See if you can help if he or she needs to do better work…like going over spelling words or listening to reading.

❏ *Sense of Power* ❏ *Respect for Others*
- **TALK WITH THE CHILD ABOUT HIS OR HER SCHOOL FRIENDS AND WHAT THEY DO TOGETHER.**
1. Talk about school recess today. "What did you play at recess?", "Who did you play with?"
2. Try to ask about these friends by name on other days. "Did you play with John today?"
3. Ask the child if the other children are nice to him or her.
4. Ask if he or she has a best friend.
5. "Why do you like to be with him or her?"

❏ Trust ❏ Acceptance

● **TAKE TIME TO LISTEN TO THE CHILD.**

1. Find a place to talk where you and the child are alone.
2. Listen to what the child says. He or she may tell you something that is making him or her unhappy.
3. Do not rush. Take time to talk together.
4. You may ask one or two things so that the child will start to talk.
5. When you talk, do not tell that you think he or she was right or wrong, but just talk about what he or she told you.
6. If you know the child is upset but does not want to talk about it, do not push him or her to tell you. Let the child know that you will be happy to hear about it when he or she wants to tell you about it. What the child may not be able to talk about today, might be talked about tomorrow.

❏ Responsibility

● **THE CHILD SHOULD LEARN TO TAKE HIS OR HER PLATE AND SILVERWARE TO THE SINK AFTER EATING.**

1. After eating, tell the child that he or she is now big and can take his or her things off the table.
2. Pick up your plate and silverware. Tell what you are doing. Take them to the sink.
3. Tell the child to do the same with his or her things. Help him or her do this if you need to.
4. Praise the child for this work.
5. Tell the child to do this every time after eating.
6. When the child does this job without you telling him or her to do it, be sure to praise.
7. Tell the family what a good job the child is doing.

❏ *Responsibility*
● **THE CHILD SHOULD LEARN TO TAKE HIS OR HER PLATE AND SILVERWARE TO THE SINK AFTER EATING.**
1. After eating, tell the child that he or she is now big and can take his or her things off the table.
2. Pick up your plate and silverware. Tell what you are doing. Take them to the sink.
3. Tell the child to do the same with his or her things. Help him or her do this if you need to.
4. Praise the child for this work.
5. Tell the child to do this every time after eating.
6. When the child does this job without you telling him or her to do it, be sure to praise.
7. Tell the family what a good job the child is doing.

❏ *Sense of Importance*
● **TRY TO FIND OUT THE THINGS THE CHILD LIKES TO DO OR WHAT HE OR SHE WANTS TO LEARN ABOUT. (THIS IS SOMETHING THE CHILD IS INTERESTED IN.)**
1. Talk with the child about his or her interest. An interest may last only one week and then he or she may have a new interest. This is okay.
2. If the child does not have an interest, try to help him or her find one. His or her interest may be animals, cars, trains, airplanes, plants, sports, and so on.
3. Some things you can do to help the child with his or her interest:
   > Go to the library with him or her for books.
   > Find magazine or newspaper articles.
   > Read the article to the child.
   > Go to places like the zoo, museum, nature center, and so on.

❏ *Acceptance* ❏ *Respect for Others*
● **WATCH AN "EDUCATIONAL" TV SHOW WITH THE CHILD.**
1. Pick out the TV show.
2. Let everyone in the family know about the show. Try to have most of them watch it with you.
3. Try not to do anything else while the TV show is on.
4. When the show is over, talk about what you saw with the child. Be sure he or she tells what he or she liked or didn't like about it. Do this for two or three minutes.
5. Thank the child for telling you his or her feelings. Anything he or she feels is okay.

❏ *Pride* ❏ *Sense of Importance*
● **ASK THE CHILD TO HELP YOU READ A STORY.**
1. Ask if the child wants to help you read to a doll, pet, pretend friend, someone older, or a young child.
2. Let him or her pick out the book to read.
3. Start to read. He or she can talk about the story or pictures as you read, or may read some words with you.
4. Praise the child for the help.
5. He or she may not want to read a book but may be happy to tell a story he or she heard (maybe from school). Praise the child for doing this.
6. Keep doing this. The child will learn to like to read.

❏ *Sense of Power* ❏ *Pride*
❏ *Sense of Importance*
● **YOU AND THE CHILD SHOULD DO SOMETHING OUTSIDE ONE OR TWO TIMES A WEEK.**
1. Some things you could do: picnic on the porch or in the park, watch the child skateboard, push him or her on a swing, take a walk, play in the yard or playground.
2. Let the child make the plans and tell you what to do.
3. Let the child know that you like doing these things.

❏ *Responsibility* ❏ *Self-respect* ❏ *Pride*
● **HELP THE CHILD LEARN TO BRUSH HIS OR HER TEETH, COMB HIS OR HER HAIR, AND DRESS BEFORE GOING TO SCHOOL.**
1. The child should learn one of these at a time. When it can be done without help, work on the next thing.
2. Get the child up early enough in the morning so there is time to do these things and not rush.
3. Have the toothbrush, toothpaste, hairbrush, comb, and clothes for school where the child can get them.
4. Tell the child that he or she is big and can brush his or her teeth. Help and watch him or her do this. When the child is good at it, tell him or her it is his or her job to do it every day.
5. Praise the child for doing this on his or her own. Let the family praise him or her.
6. Go on to the next thing—taking care of his or her hair, or putting on clothes.

❏ *Sense of Power* ❏ *Responsibility*
❏ *Pride* ❏ *Sense of Importance*

● **HELP THE CHILD PICK OUT HIS OR HER CLOTHES.**

1. Show the child which clothes look nice together. Show which colors go well together. Praise when the child does this.
2. Tell the child "You want to look nice. It makes you feel good when you do and when your friends like the way you look."
3. Praise him or her by saying, "You did a nice job dressing today.", "I like the way you combed your hair.", "That shirt and pants look nice together."

❏ *Sense of Power* ❏ *Responsibility*
❏ *Pride* ❏ *Sense of Importance*

● **THE CHILD LEARNS TO HANG UP HIS OR HER COAT AND PUT SCHOOL PAPERS AND BOOKS WHERE THEY SHOULD BE.**

1. Tell the child, "You are bigger and can do some things by yourself."
2. Show where to put the coat, papers and books. Tell the child that you like to see his or her work.
3. Help the child do this every day after school.
4. Let the child show you some papers. Talk about the work. Do this about the same time each day.
5. When he or she hangs up the coat and puts school work away with no help, praise the child.

❏ *Acceptance* ❏ *Responsibility* ❏ *Pride*

● **TALK WITH THE CHILD ABOUT HIS OR HER SCHOOL PAPERS EACH DAY.**

1. Let the child know that you like to hear about the school work and see the papers.
2. Talk about the work. Tell what you think is good about the work. Praise the work that is right.
3. See if you can help if he or she needs to do better work...like going over spelling words or listening to reading.

❏ *Sense of Power* ❏ *Respect for Others*

● **TALK WITH THE CHILD ABOUT HIS OR HER SCHOOL FRIENDS AND WHAT THEY DO TOGETHER.**

1. Talk about school recess today. "What did you play at recess?", "Who did you play with?"
2. Try to ask about these friends by name on other days. "Did you play with John today?"
3. Ask the child if the other children are nice to him or her.
4. Ask if he or she has a best friend.
5. "Why do you like to be with him or her?"

❏ *Trust* ❏ *Acceptance*

● **TAKE TIME TO LISTEN TO THE CHILD.**

1. Find a place to talk where you and the child are alone.
2. Listen to what the child says. He or she may tell you something that is making him or her unhappy.
3. Do not rush. Take time to talk together.
4. You may ask one or two things so that the child will start to talk.
5. When you talk, do not tell that you think he or she was right or wrong, but just talk about what he or she told you.
6. If you know the child is upset but does not want to talk about it, do not push him or her to tell you. Let the child know that you will be happy to hear about it when he or she wants to tell you about it. What the child may not be able to talk about today, might be talked about tomorrow.

READ CAREFULLY BEFORE YOU DO THIS EXERCISE WITH THE CHILD OR CLASS.

❏ *Sense of Importance*

● **RELAXATION (Getting in touch with yourself—taking control of YOU!)**
(Suggestion: This is a great "after recess" exercise for the entire class. It can be a relaxer for everyone!)
Teacher: "This works when you feel upset, mad, or tired. It can get you back IN TOUCH with yourself—you can be in control of you!"

1. Sit straight in your chair, feet flat on the floor.
2. Close your eyes or look down into your lap.
3. Breathe IN through your nose and let it OUT slowly through your mouth.
4. Again...slowly...IN through your nose...OUT through your mouth.
5. Again...take in as much air as you can...till you can't take in another drop.
6. Let it OUT slowly...slowly...until there's not a drop of air left.
7. Repeat this six times.
8. Then begin to breathe normally again.
9. RELAX...enjoy the feeling (10 seconds).
10. Open your eyes.

OPTION: Show interest in a "special interest" of the child.

❏ *Sense of Importance*

● **TRY TO FIND OUT THE THINGS THE CHILD LIKES TO DO OR WHAT HE OR SHE WANTS TO LEARN ABOUT. (THIS IS SOMETHING THE CHILD IS INTERESTED IN.)**

1. Talk with the child about his or her interest. An interest may last only one week and then he or she may have a new interest. This is okay.
2. If the child does not have an interest, try to help him or her find one. His or her interest may be animals, cars, trains, airplanes, plants, sports, and so on.
3. Some things you can do to help the child with his or her interest:
   Go to the library with him or her for books.
   Find magazine or newspaper articles.
   Read the article to the child.
   Go to places like the zoo, museum, nature center, and so on.

❑ Trust ❑ Acceptance

● **TAKE TIME TO LISTEN TO THE CHILD.**
1. Find a place to talk where you and the child are alone.
2. Listen to what the child says. He or she may tell you something that is making him or her unhappy.
3. Do not rush. Take time to talk together.
4. You may ask one or two things so that the child will start to talk.
5. When you talk, do not tell that you think he or she was right or wrong, but just talk about what he or she told you.
6. If you know the child is upset but does not want to talk about it, do not push him or her to tell you. Let the child know that you will be happy to hear about it when he or she wants to tell you about it. What the child may not be able to talk about today, might be talked about tomorrow.

❑ Sense of Importance

● **TRY TO FIND OUT THE THINGS THE CHILD LIKES TO DO OR WHAT HE OR SHE WANTS TO LEARN ABOUT. (THIS IS SOMETHING THE CHILD IS INTERESTED IN.)**
1. Talk with the child about his or her interest. An interest may last only one week and then he or she may have a new interest. This is okay.
2. If the child does not have an interest, try to help him or her find one. His or her interest may be animals, cars, trains, airplanes, plants, sports, and so on.
3. Some things you can do to help the child with his or her interest:
   Go to the library with him or her for books.
   Find magazine or newspaper articles.
   Read the article to the child.
   Go to places like the zoo, museum, nature center, and so on.

❑ Acceptance ❑ Responsibility ❑ Pride

● **YOU SHOULD TALK WITH THE CHILD ABOUT HIS OR HER SCHOOL PAPERS.**
1. Let the child know that you like to hear about the school work and see the papers.
2. Talk about the work. Tell what you think is good about the work. Praise the work that is right.
3. See if you can help if he or she needs to do better work…like going over spelling words or listening to reading.

❑ Pride ❑ Sense of Importance

● **ASK THE CHILD TO HELP YOU READ A STORY.**
1. Ask if the child wants to help you read to a doll, pet, pretend friend, someone older, or a young child.
2. Let him or her pick out the book to read.
3. Start to read. He or she can talk about the story or pictures as you read, or may read some words with you.
4. Praise the child for the help.
5. He or she may not want to read a book but may be happy to tell a story he or she heard (maybe from school). Praise the child for doing this.
6. Keep doing this. The child will learn to like to read.

❑ Sense of Power ❑ Respect for Others

● **TALK WITH THE CHILD ABOUT HIS OR HER SCHOOL FRIENDS AND WHAT THEY DO TOGETHER.**
1. Talk about school recess today. "What did you play at recess?", "Who did you play with?"
2. Try to ask about these friends by name on other days. "Did you play with John today?"
3. Ask the child if the other children are nice to him or her.
4. Ask if he or she has a best friend.
5. "Why do you like to be with him or her?"

Level 10 Characteristics

- Concerned with "Why?"
- Separation between the sexes, same sex friendships predominate
- Teasing/chasing
- Curious, may have hobbies or collections
- Likes to barter or trade
- Interested in people; friendly, and cooperative
- Likes to be included in adult gatherings
- Sense of personal history
- Likes dramatic role-playing
- Impact of social status (clothing/appearance, etc.)
- Helpfulness depends on the mood
- Concerned with how caregiver/adults perceive him or her
- Beginning of difference between home and public behavior
- School means friends
- School attendance is good
- Less concerned with teacher and more with the "group"
- Gossips
- Begins to question parental behavior
- Impatient
- Bursts of emotion/changeable emotions
- Self-directed: chooses and completes own activities better
- Getting a sense of who he or she is
- Sense of fairness
- Increasing awareness of own behaviors and emotions
- More self-confident and responsible
- Increasing self-control and able to resist external pressures
- Less quarreling with parents and more accommodating
- Self-derogatory remarks
- Achievement is important
- Hero worship

Level 10 Information

Self-esteem is a feeling.
If you have HIGH self-esteem...
> You make good friends!
> You care about yourself and other people;
> You are responsible;
> You enjoy learning;
> You are proud of what you do;
> You can handle failure;
> You can share feelings.

HIGH self-esteem is having a GOOD feeling about yourself, your place in the family, your school, and your world.

THINGS TO REMEMBER:

- When you first see the child after school or work and the child has done something wrong and you are upset, try to say at least 2 GOOD THINGS to him or her BEFORE you talk about any bad things.
- If the child is not doing the activity right...it's okay and the child is okay...and you are okay! There is no right or wrong.
- Use the child's name when talking to him or her.
- Children take things in their life SERIOUSLY. You should, too. This shows RESPECT for the child.
- Same bed time and bath time EVERY night.
- Do not walk around the house nude.
- Do not use foul language in front of the child.
- Keep adult sexual activity private.
- KEEP TRYING!
- LOOK for the Good Stuff!
- FIND A REASON TO SAY EACH OF THESE PHRASES ONCE A DAY:
  You are doing a good job.
  Good work!
  I'm proud of you.

DON'T GIVE UP!

— If the child does not want to do the activity with you the way you want him or her to...try again tomorrow.

— Keep trying. This is the way you **SHOW** the child that you mean what you say. A child needs to **TRUST** in order to share with you or listen to you.

— **HOW** you say something is sometimes more important than **WHAT** you say.

You may be doing MOST of these things already as part of the way you care for children and run your home. By doing these things in the way they are written, you will be helping the child's self-esteem **plus** your own self-esteem.

When you can help somebody feel good... you feel good!

"I" messages let the child know exactly what you want, why you want it, and how you want it. The child does not have to GUESS what you want or how you feel. This is a way of setting LIMITS. Some examples are:

- "**I** feel very upset when you throw your clothes on the floor. Clothes cost money... **I** work hard for my money and **I** want you to have nice clothes to wear."
- "**I** do not want you to carry those two full glasses of milk at one time. **I** am afraid they will spill."

The BASE program is about helping children have HIGH self-esteem. It is a group of things to do and share with a child. These things are short, simple and positive. They should be done everyday when possible.

REMEMBER:

If any of these things do not agree with the way you believe or your religion (example: dancing), do not do it.

Level 10 Human Awareness

Here are some things for you to talk about with your child. It means a lot for you to let the child know that you want to talk about these things.

BOTH PARENTS SHOULD PARTICIPATE. When possible, both parents should share the responsibility for sex education. Men have expected most sex education to be done by the mother. When both parents participate, the child sees sex education as a family affair.

What you should say when the child asks you something:
    Always answer. Do not wait to tell what he or she wants to know, even if it seems that he or she is asking in order to shock you. Do not say, "I'll tell you when you are older". Answer in the right way and with good information for the child's age. You build self-esteem when you answer. If you *do not* tell what he or she wants to know, the child learns: 1. not to ask you things; or, 2. that he or she is not "big" enough or "good" enough; or, 3. that you do not think the questions are important.

What should you do about four-letter words?
    Children often use four-letter words to find out what they mean, or to see what adults will do. Do not be shocked at this, but try to teach the child at this time. Say the four-letter word back to him or her. This will show that you are not shocked or that saying the "dirty" word is not so great. Ask the child to tell you what the word means. Listen and then say what it means and how you feel about the way it was used. This is a time for you to tell him or her what your values are, how you think about things, or what is right or wrong.

Telling children about sex will not make them think more about it. It will not lead them to experimenting or trying to do it.

Talk about people. When a child wants to know about the body or how babies are made, he or she is thinking about people. When you answer the questions by talking about cats and dogs, the child will not think that it is the same in people.

Children want short answers that are to the point.

Don't be afraid to say, "I don't know". You should then try to find the answer. There are books about this that the child can understand. First read the book by yourself so that you know what is in it. Then read it *with* the child.

Be sure you know what your own values are...how you think about things...what is right or wrong.

It is okay to talk together about different ways of thinking; ways that may be different from the way you may feel.

Let the child know that you want to be asked questions and will answer them. Don't say, "I'll tell you when you're older." Try to teach when things happen (like on TV, or radio, in newspapers, or magazines), with your friends, other children, or someone in the family.

Let the child know that it is normal and okay for there to be changes in his or her body.

Keep your sense of humor.

(continued...)

Don't try to be perfect. No one is always right.

Some children do not ask questions. This does not mean the child doesn't have any questions. He or she may think about many things and have the wrong idea or wrong information about what he or she is thinking about.

DON'T WAIT FOR THE CHILD TO ASK!
If he or she isn't asking questions about sex, it may be because the child got the feeling from you that you don't talk about sex in your home. It is your job to see that he or she knows the right things about sex, and does not have wrong information.

When you talk about sex, don't talk to the boys alone or girls alone. Boys and girls need to know how the other's body works. Boys will be living around women all their lives. They need to know about ovulation, contraception (how to keep from getting pregnant or sexual diseases), and menstruation (the period or "curse"). Girls also need to know how the man's body works. You want to be sure they learn that sex is something that the family can talk about.

When you talk about something that is hard for you, it is okay to say, "This makes me uncomfortable, but because I love you, it's something we need to talk about". The child might be just as uncomfortable or as embarrassed as you are!

Some questions may shock you, but you should be sure to answer them. If not, the child may ask someone else and he or she may not have your values or know the facts. When the child asks shocking questions about contraceptives or oral sex, he or she is letting you know that he or she trusts you.

If the child talks about things that make you think he or she may have been sexually abused, contact your pediatrician, clinic, or phone a child abuse hotline.

When the child asks questions that you don't have answers for, ask your family doctor, clinic, or health department.

REMEMBER:
If anything written here is against your religious or moral beliefs, don't do it!

Level 10 Teacher Information

(To be used with **C** Exercises)

Your cooperation with these exercises is VERY IMPORTANT.

As you know, success or failure in school is directly tied to self-esteem. The intelligent child with low self-esteem will do poorly in school...the average child with HIGH self-esteem will generally be successful.

It's also true that low self-esteem gets in the way of good performance and that bad performance reinforces low self-esteem.

This exercise can be done with the child alone in the beginning. Within a week or so, you might want to share it with the entire class. This exercise works very well as a "calmer downer" after recess, or break.

This is a way of trying to show a little **extra special attention** to a child who is very much in need of POSITIVE strokes.

Look for the POSITIVE and PRAISE it.
Use the child's name when giving PRAISE.
Be specific with the PRAISE.

Your support is appreciated!

❏ *Acceptance* ❏ *Responsibility* ❏ *Pride*
● **EVERYONE IN THE FAMILY MUST DO SOME JOBS AROUND THE HOUSE. SOME JOBS MAY CHANGE AFTER A WEEK.**
1. Kinds of things to be done: empty trash, sweep kitchen floor, clean bathrooms, pick up living or family room, make bed, clean bedroom, wash or dry dishes, put dirty clothes away and so on. Show the child how you want the job to be done.
2. Look at the work the child did.
   A. Be sure to tell what was done right.
   B. If something was done wrong or could be a little better, tell the child what could have been done. You may want to do the job with the child so that he or she can see how you want it done.

❏ *Approval* ❏ *Pride*
❏ *Responsibility* ❏ *Sense of Importance*
● **HAVE THE CHILD HELP PLAN AND SHOP FOR A MEAL.**
1. Have the child help you plan a meal.
2. Together, plan the things you need to make this meal. Make a list of things to buy.
3. Take the child to the store. Let him or her help find the things that are on the list.
4. Let the child fix part of this meal, such as fix the salad, wash potatoes, or any other thing you think he or she can do okay.
5. Praise the child for picking out such a good meal and for the help. Make sure other family members know that the child helped. (Suggestion: It is best to do this with one child at a time.)

❏ *Approval* ❏ *Sense of Importance*
● **GIVE THE CHILD HELP WITH HIS OR HER HOBBY.**
1. Your child may need some money for the hobby, such as bowling. (You may want to help him or her find a hobby that does not need much money.)
2. Be sure the child knows that you like him or her to work on the hobby and that you will help in any way you can.
3. Help work on the hobby by taking the child to the library for books to read.
4. Save pictures and stories about the hobby that are in the newspaper or magazines to give to him or her.

5. Help the child make a scrapbook, or a group of pictures pasted together (collage) about the hobby. He or she should look in the newspaper, magazines, and books for things about the hobby.

❏ *Approval* ❏ *Sense of Power*
❏ *Acceptance* ❏ *Respect for Others*
● **TRY TO GET TO KNOW THE CHILD'S FRIENDS.**
1. Have the child ask a friend over to your house after school if it is okay with the friend's parent.
2. After you get to know the friend, ask if he or she could do some things with the family—have dinner, go shopping, play ball, and so on.
3. Tell your child when he or she is with the friend that you like this friend. "I'm so glad that [friend's name] came to see you and likes to do things with our family."

❏ *Acceptance*
● **TALK ABOUT TRADITIONS, THINGS THAT THE FAMILY ALWAYS DOES AND HAS DONE IN THE PAST. (GOOD TO DO AROUND HOLIDAYS OR SPECIAL DAYS.)**
1. Take the child to the library. Find books on traditions: holidays, religious, social, those for your state or part of the country.
2. The child can think about the family traditions while he reads the books.
3. You and the child can visit museums, exhibits, shopping centers, and so on when they have something for special holidays.
4. The child can help decorate the home for some holidays.
5. Talk about everyone's traditions. What things were done in the past, now, and in your family.
6. Have the child tell you what he or she would like to do as a family tradition.
7. Make a "new" tradition for your family to do from now on.

❏ *Sense of Importance*
● **TRY TO HAVE THE CHILD BECOME A PART OF A GROUP.**
1. Some ideas of groups for children this age that work on different things of interest: Girl Scouts, Boy Scouts, Camp Fire, church, athletics, 4H, music or theater groups.
2. The people in charge of the group must encourage and *support* the child in this effort.

❏ *Responsibility* ❏ *Self-respect*

● **THE CHILD NEEDS TO HAVE GOOD HABITS KEEPING THE BODY AND HAIR CLEAN.**

1. Each day the child should:
   A. Use his or her own toothbrush and paste.
   B. Wash hands and face.
   C. Brush, comb, or pick hair to make it neat.
   D. Change underwear each day.
2. Every one or two days take a shower or bath and wash hair. When it is warmer outside, this should be done every day. *It is important for the child to take a bath and go to bed at about the same time every day.*

❏ *Trust* ❏ *Acceptance*

● **TALK TOGETHER AS A FAMILY AT MEALTIME.**

1. Each person, if he or she wants, should be able to talk about something that happened that day.
2. Try to talk about good things.
3. When someone is talking, the others should not make him or her feel bad about what is said. No "put downs"!

❏ *Trust*

● **TALK WITH THE CHILD ABOUT FAMILIES.**

1. Meal time may be a good time to talk.
2. Things you want the child to know:
   A. Families may be made up in different ways. There may be only a father or mother. A family may have grandparents, aunts, cousins, and so on. A family may be a stepfather or stepmother with children, so there are stepbrothers and stepsisters.
   B. No one kind of family is best. All kinds can be okay.
   C. Every family has different rules, and that's okay. No set of rules is best or right. Everyone in the family must live by their own family rules.
3. Ways to help the child when he or she says something about the different ones in the family:
   A. Everyone in the family can be different and have different things happen in their life. This is okay.
   B. You should not say that one child is better than the other in any way. They may be different, but don't let them get the feeling that he or she is better, or not as good.

❏ *Trust* ❏ *Self-respect*

● **TALK ABOUT SCHOOL WORK WITH THE CHILD AND SEE THAT THE HOMEWORK IS DONE.**

1. A. Say something good about his or her home work, like "I'm glad you came home with your English work today."
   B. Ask the child to tell you what went on in school today…was the work hard?
   C. Ask to see any papers he or she came home with.
   D. Talk about the work that was done right. Have the child go over the papers and fix anything that was wrong. He or she should bring them back to the teacher the next day.
2. Plan a special time for homework—before or after dinner, before TV and so on.
3. He or she needs a place to study.
   A. There must be a table and chair. (He or she should not be on the floor by the TV)
   B. You should keep it quiet when he or she is doing homework.
4. Ask about the work. See if you can give help with anything. "I think you do so well in spelling. How are you doing in math?"
5. When the child needs help, it is sometimes good to say, "Ask your teacher. I'd like to know what he or she says about it." You must also ask the teacher about how the child is doing in school.
6. Let the child know that you feel school is very *important* and that you care about what he or she is learning.

❏ *Responsibility* ❏ *Self-respect*

● **HAVE THE CHILD SPEND SOME TIME READING.**

1. Let the child pick out what to read. It may be something about his or her hobby, sports, and so on.
2. It should be for 10 to 20 minutes, and at about the *same time* every day or every other day.
3. Try to get the child to talk about what he or she read…to share with you.
4. Give the child a reward that you both picked out for doing this. It may be extra TV time, something to eat, or anything special to him or her.

❏ *Trust* ❏ *Responsibility* ❏ *Pride*

● **THE CHILD NEEDS TO LEARN TO MAKE THE BED AND PUT DIRTY CLOTHES AWAY.**

1. When dirty clothes are taken off, they should be put in the *right* place, not around the room.

2. Dirty sheets and towels should be put in the *right* place on the day the family changes bedding. You may have to tell the child to do this until he or she does it on his or her own.

3. Make a rule when the bed should be made on school days (make before school), holidays (made before playing or TV). You should check the bed and talk about how it looks. Praise the child for doing it without being told to do so.

❑ *Responsibility* ❑ *Self-respect*

● **THE CHILD NEEDS TO HAVE GOOD HABITS KEEPING THE BODY AND HAIR CLEAN.**

1. Each day the child should:
   A. Use his or her own toothbrush and paste.
   B. Wash hands and face.
   C. Brush, comb, or pick hair to make it neat.
   D. Change underwear each day.
2. Every one or two days take a shower or bath and wash hair. When it is warmer outside, this should be done every day. *It is important for the child to take a bath and go to bed at about the same time every day.*

❑ *Trust* ❑ *Acceptance*

● **TALK TOGETHER AS A FAMILY AT MEALTIME.**

1. Each person, if he or she wants, should be able to talk about something that happened that day.
2. Try to talk about good things.
3. When someone is talking, the others should not make him or her feel bad about what is said. No "put downs"!

❑ *Trust* ❑ *Responsibility* ❑ *Pride*

● **THE CHILD NEEDS TO LEARN TO MAKE THE BED AND PUT DIRTY CLOTHES AWAY.**

1. When dirty clothes are taken off, they should be put in the *right* place, not around the room.
2. Dirty sheets and towels should be put in the *right* place on the day the family changes bedding. You may have to tell the child to do this until he or she does it on his or her own.
3. Make a rule when the bed should be made on school days (make before school), holidays (made before playing or TV). You should check the bed and talk about how it looks. Praise the child for doing it without being told to do so.

❑ *Acceptance* ❑ *Responsibility* ❑ *Pride*

● **EVERYONE IN THE FAMILY MUST DO SOME JOBS AROUND THE HOUSE. SOME JOBS MAY CHANGE AFTER A WEEK.**

1. Kinds of things to be done: empty trash, sweep kitchen floor, clean bathrooms, pick up living or family room, make bed, clean bedroom, wash or dry dishes, put dirty clothes away and so on. Show the child how you want the job to be done.
2. Look at the work the child did.
   A. Be sure to tell what was done right.
   B. If something was done wrong or could be a little better, tell the child what could have been done. You may want to do the job with the child so that he or she can see how you want it done.

❑ *Approval* ❑ *Sense of Importance*

● **GIVE THE CHILD HELP WITH HIS OR HER HOBBY.**

1. Your child may need some money for the hobby, such as bowling. (You may want to help him or her find a hobby that does not need much money.)
2. Be sure the child knows that you like him or her to work on the hobby and that you will help in any way you can.
3. Help work on the hobby by taking the child to the library for books to read.
4. Save pictures and stories about the hobby that are in the newspaper or magazines to give to him or her.
5. Help the child make a scrapbook, or a group of pictures pasted together (collage) about the hobby. He or she should look in the newspaper, magazines, and books for things about the hobby.

READ CAREFULLY BEFORE YOU DO THIS EXERCISE WITH THE CHILD OR CLASS.

❑ *Trust*

● **SOMETHING TO DO TO HELP YOU RELAX.**

1. Sit up straight on a chair like a stiff board, feet flat on the floor.
2. Close your eyes or look into your lap.
3. "This is something you can do anytime, any place, when you feel upset or angry! This is a way to get back in control of you!"
4. Make a fist with your right hand, hold it tight, tighter, now let go and relax. Do the same with the left hand.
5. Sit up straight, straighter, push your feet flat into the floor. Relax!
6. Pull in your stomach, hold it in, tight, tighter! Relax!
7. Bring your chin down toward your chest. Feel the muscles pulling in the front of your neck.
8. Move your head back toward the back of the chair. Feel the muscles in front of your neck.
9. Do numbers seven and eight for three times.
10. Tighten all the muscles in your whole body, tight, tighter, tighter!
11. Now—HANG LOOSE!
12. Do numbers ten and eleven for three times.
13. Now RELAX. Sit still and listen to what's around you. Listen for all the different sounds you can hear in the "quiet".

TEACHER'S OPTION:

1. Encourage children to ask for help when needed.
2. Use "I" statements when dealing with judgments or comments to children:
"I like the way you did that..."
"I appreciated what you said about..."

❏ Sense of Importance ❏ Acceptance

● **TALK WITH THE CHILD ABOUT THINGS THE FAMILY DOES TOGETHER.**
1. Find a place to talk where no one is around.
2. Try to get the child to talk about his or her family.
3. Ask what he or she likes to do best with the family. What besides watching TV?
4. What other things would he or she like to do with the family?
5. You may want to share some of your own family experiences, family jokes, and traditions.

❏ Approval ❏ Sense of Power
❏ Sense of Importance

● **HAVE THE CHILD TALK ABOUT WHAT HE OR SHE THINKS.**
1. Try to have the child talk about his or her interests, hobbies, sports, cartoons, movies, TV, musicians.
2. Ask what the child thinks is good about the person he or she like in sports, and so on.
3. If you also like the person, hobby, or interest, be sure to tell him or her that you do.

❏ Sense of Power ❏ Self-respect

● **SOME ACTIVITIES TO DO THAT SHOW THE CHILD THAT HE OR SHE CAN WORK TO GET BETTER AT DOING SOMETHING. CHOOSE 1 (OR 2) OF THESE ACTIVITIES. PRAISE THE CHILD FOR GETTING BETTER OR EVEN STAYING THE SAME. DO IT WHENEVER YOU GET TOGETHER.**
1. Throw a ball.
2. Run faster and farther.
3. Jump higher and farther.
4. Learn a new spelling word each day.
5. See how tall he or she is. How much did he or she grow? (one time every 4 weeks)

❏ Approval ❏ Sense of Power
❏ Sense of Importance

● **PLAY A GAME TOGETHER.**
1. Take turns picking the game you will play. It could be a reward for the child to pick the game.
2. Pick a time to play the game when it is not homework time.
3. The game can be played at a table or outside, like touch football, catch, badminton, and so on.

5th-6th grade

Level 11 Characteristics

- Exaggerated emotions may be expressed
- Girls are taller/heavier—more sexually advanced and concerned about their bodies
- Better relationships and increased trust with adults
- More conscious and judgmental of own appearance
- Likes family activities and willing to participate
- Conforming to peer expectations
- Has secret codes, meeting places, cliques, etc.
- Able to be responsible
- Accepts teacher's authority (if he or she is fair and not strict)
- Teamwork possible

- Increased activity and appetite
- Needs to be noticed
- Independence from parents begins and child may challenge authority
- Friends chosen by mutual interest
- Admits interest in opposite sex
- Teases and shows off for opposite sex
- Shows off learning skills
- Money can mean independence
- Conforming to increase of society's expectations
- Possible experimentation with sex, drugs, and alcohol
- Attempting to conform to societal and peer expectations (which may be in conflict)

Level 11 Information

Self-esteem is a feeling.
If you have HIGH self-esteem...
>   You make good friends!
>   You care about yourself and other people;
>   You are responsible;
>   You enjoy learning;
>   You are proud of what you do;
>   You can handle failure;
>   You can share feelings.

HIGH self-esteem is having a GOOD feeling about yourself, your place in the family, your school, and your world.

THINGS TO REMEMBER:

- When you first see the child after school or work and the child has done something wrong and you are upset, try to say at least 2 GOOD THINGS to him or her BEFORE you talk about any bad things.
- If the child is not doing the activity right...it's okay and the child is okay...and you are okay! There is no right or wrong.
- Use the child's name when talking to him or her.
- Children take things in their life SERIOUSLY. You should, too. This shows RESPECT for the child.
- Same bed time and bath time EVERY night.
- Do not walk around the house nude.
- Do not use foul language in front of the child.
- Keep adult sexual activity private.
- KEEP TRYING!
- LOOK for the Good Stuff!
- FIND A REASON TO SAY EACH OF THESE PHRASES ONCE A DAY:
  You are doing a good job.
  Good work!
  I'm proud of you.

DON'T GIVE UP!

— If the child does not want to do the activity with you the way you want him or her to...try again tomorrow.
— Keep trying. This is the way you **SHOW** the child that you mean what you say. A child needs to **TRUST** in order to share with you or listen to you.
— **HOW** you say something is sometimes more important than **WHAT** you say.

You may be doing MOST of these things already as part of the way you care for children and run your home. By doing these things in the way they are written, you will be helping the child's self-esteem **plus** your own self-esteem.

When you can help somebody feel good... you feel good!

"I" messages let the child know exactly what you want, why you want it, and how you want it. The child does not have to GUESS what you want or how you feel. This is a way of setting LIMITS. Some examples are:

- "**I** feel very upset when you throw your clothes on the floor. Clothes cost money... **I** work hard for my money and **I** want you to have nice clothes to wear."
- "**I** do not want you to carry those two full glasses of milk at one time. **I** am afraid they will spill."

The BASE program is about helping children have HIGH self-esteem. It is a group of things to do and share with a child. These things are short, simple and positive. They should be done everyday when possible.

REMEMBER:

If any of these things do not agree with the way you believe or your religion (example: dancing), do not do it.

Here are some things for you to talk about with your child. It means a lot for you to let the child know that you want to talk about these things.

BOTH PARENTS SHOULD PARTICIPATE. When possible, both parents should share the responsibility for sex education. Men have expected most sex education to be done by the mother. When both parents participate, the child sees sex education as a family affair.

What should you do about four-letter words?

Children often use four-letter words to find out what they mean, or to see what adults will do. Do not be shocked at this, but try to teach the child at this time. Say the four-letter word back to him or her. This will show that you are not shocked or that saying the "dirty" word is not so great. Ask the child to tell you what the word means. Listen and then say what it means and how you feel about the way it was used. This is a time for you to tell him or her what your values are, how you think about things, or what is right or wrong.

Telling children about sex will not make them think more about it. It will not lead them to experimenting or trying to do it.

Don't be afraid to say, "I don't know". You should then try to find the answer. There are books about this that the child can understand. First read the book by yourself so that you know what is in it. Then read it with the child.

Be sure you know what your own values are…how you think about things…what is right or wrong.

It is okay to talk together about different ways of thinking; ways that may be different from the way you may feel.

Let the child know that you want to be asked questions and will answer them. Don't say, "I'll tell you when you're older." Try to teach when things happen (like on TV, or radio, in newspapers, or magazines), with your friends, other children, or someone in the family.

Let the child know that it is normal and okay for there to be changes in his or her body.

Keep your sense of humor.

Don't try to be perfect. No one is always right.

Some children do not ask questions. This does not mean the child doesn't have any questions. He or she may think about many things and have the wrong idea or wrong information about what he or she is thinking about

DON'T WAIT FOR THE CHILD TO ASK! If he or she isn't asking questions about sex, it may be because the child got the feeling from you that you don't talk about sex in your home. It is your job to see that he or she knows the right things about sex, and does not have wrong information.

When you talk about sex, don't talk to the boys alone or girls alone. Boys and girls need to know how the other's body works. Boys will be living around women all their lives. They need to know about ovulation, contraception (how to keep from getting pregnant or sexual diseases),

(continued…)

Level 11 Human Awareness

and menstruation (the period or "curse"). Girls also need to know how the man's body works. You want to be sure they learn that sex is something that the family can talk about.

When you talk about something that is hard for you, it is okay to say, "This makes me uncomfortable, but because I love you, it's something we need to talk about". The child might be just as uncomfortable or as embarrassed as you are!

Some questions may shock you, but you should be sure to answer them. If not, the child may ask someone else and he or she may not have your values or know the facts. When the child asks shocking questions about contraceptives or oral sex, he or she is letting you know that he or she trusts you.

How to get the child to ask questions about his or her body changing.

You may say, "I see that your body is starting to change. If you have any questions or if there is something you're wondering about, I'm here." Let the child know that it is your job, because you ar the parent, to help and guide him or her to understand questions about life, his or her body, sex, and making good choices in what you do and say. "We all think about sex, some thoughts are good and some are bad, but this is normal and okay. If you want to talk about it, I am here. Come to me any time."

Tell the child what is "normal"…
1. Changes in the body are normal, but everyone's body doesn't change at the same time. Boys and girls grow at different speeds, some slower and some faster. In some, hormones may be starting to "take over your body" so wet dreams are normal, irregular periods are normal, and so on.
2. Tell the child that there are many ways to show affection, love and caring. Intercourse is *only one* of the many ways. Other ways can be hugging and kissing. Talking together can also be intimate.
3. It is important to teach the child to make good choices in what he or she does and says. Help the child to learn what will happen when you do some things. Teaching how to make a good choice is better for your child than making demands and threats. You cannot be with your child every minute.
4. Let the child know that some people, when they are dating, have sex so that they can "use" someone, and that can really hurt a boy or girl.

If the child talks about things that make you think he or she may have been sexually abused, contact your pediatrician, clinic, or phone a child abuse hotline.

When the child asks questions that you don't have answers for, ask your family doctor, clinic, or health department.

REMEMBER:
If anything written here is against your religious or moral beliefs, don't do it!

Level 11 Teacher Information

(To be used with **C** Exercises)

Your cooperation with these exercises is VERY IMPORTANT.

As you know, success or failure in school is directly tied to self-esteem. The intelligent child with low self-esteem will do poorly in school...the average child with HIGH self-esteem will generally be successful.

It's also true that low self-esteem gets in the way of good performance and that bad performance reinforces low self-esteem.

This exercise can be done with the child alone in the beginning. Within a week or so, you might want to share it with the entire class. This exercise works very well as a "calmer downer" after recess, or break.

This is a way of trying to show a little **extra special attention** to a child who is very much in need of POSITIVE strokes.

Look for the POSITIVE and PRAISE it.
Use the child's name when giving PRAISE.
Be specific with the PRAISE.

Your support is appreciated!

❐ *Responsibility* ❐ *Self-respect* ❐ *Pride*

● **THE CHILD NEEDS TO HAVE GOOD HABITS KEEPING HIS OR HER BODY AND HAIR CLEAN.**

1. Make sure the child has the things needed for keeping clean.
2. Tell the child how often he or she needs to use these things and how to be able to tell on your own if they need to be used:
    * toothbrush—two times a day
    * deodorant—every morning
    * shower or bath—one time a day or when sweaty or dirty
    * hairbrush, comb—whenever hair looks messy
   (Show the child how to best brush or comb his or her hair and how it should look when it's done neat enough.)

❐ *Approval* ❐ *Responsibility*

● **SHOW THE CHILD THAT YOU LIKE TO KNOW ABOUT HIS OR HER HOMEWORK.**

1. Praise the child for putting the homework in the spot you both pick out. It should be placed in the same spot every day. "I'm glad you put your homework on the hall table." Tell other things you are glad the child did.
2. You may ask, "What homework do you have tonight?"
3. Plan a special time to do homework. The TV should not be on at this time.
4. Have a place at a table where written homework can be done.
5. Go over the work with the child when it is done.
6. Ask the child if he or she needs help with some work or subject. You may say something like, "I am pleased with your history quiz. Tell me about your spelling grades."
7. If needed, try to get the child to ask the teacher for help with the subject.

❐ *Trust* ❐ *Acceptance*

● **WHILE THE FAMILY EATS DINNER, IT IS GOOD TO TALK ABOUT THE DAY.**

1. When everyone has their food, Mother or Father can start by telling a good thing that happened that day or what he or she liked about the day.
2. If someone else doesn't tell something good about their day, try to get the child to do this.

3. If the child still doesn't say anything, you may tell about something good in his or her day that you saw, such as he or she brought home good papers, a friend called, he or she got along with a brother or sister, and so on.
4. When a child does share something, be sure to say something good about what he or she said.
5. Try to do this every day.

❐ *Acceptance* ❐ *Responsibility* ❐ *Pride*

● **EVERYONE IN THE FAMILY SHOULD HAVE SOME JOBS TO DO.**

1. Think of 3 daily and 3 weekly jobs to be done. The child should pick and do one from each list. Daily work may be: empty trash, dishwasher, feed and water animals, carry clean clothes to bedrooms, and so on. Weekly work may be to dust or vacuum the house, clean the bathroom, and so on.
2. Plan together for what time and day the jobs should be done.
3. Very often you may have to tell the child that, "The job must be done today!"
4. Praise the child for:
   Doing the job on his or her own
   Doing the job when you reminded him or her
   Good attitude or working willingly on the job
   Helping the family
   Taking responsibility

❐ *Acceptance*

● **THE FAMILY SHOULD PLAN TO SPEND TIME *TOGETHER*.**

1. Tell the family that you want to plan to do something together besides watching TV. Think of a time and a day of the week to do this.
2. You and the family should talk about the idea.
3. If they do not have any ideas of what to do, you may have some; such as games, puzzles, radio, dancing, quiet time, cards, going to the park or library, or going for a walk.

❐ *Responsibility* ❐ *Pride*

● **YOU MAY GROW PLANTS WITH THE CHILD.**

1. Talk about what you both want to grow: vegetables, flowers, or a plant. Talk about what needs to be done to grow them.
2. You and the child may go to the library for a book on growing vegetables, flowers, or plants. Both of you may ask someone who knows about gardens what must be done (hardware or garden store).

(continued...)

3. Fix the place for the plant. It may be the ground, a pot, or milk carton, or any other thing that is right. Be sure the plant is in the right kind of light for it to grow.
4. Plant the seed or small plant. You may use a cutting of a plant someone gave you.
5. Make a chart with the child so that he or she can do the things needed for the plant to grow: watering, turning, feeding, and so on.
6. Praise the child for the good work, and taking care of the plant when needed.
7. You *should not* see if you or the child can do a better job of growing a plant. The child should get joy out of doing this job, not see who is better.
8. If you have a camera, take a picture of him or her and the plant every week. This is a nice way for all of you to see how the plant grows.

❏ *Approval* ❏ *Responsibility*
❏ *Pride* ❏ *Sense of Importance*
● **THE CHILD CAN HELP YOU DO GROCERY SHOPPING.**
1. When you make a list, think of what you need in these food groups: dairy, bread-grains-pasta, meat and fish, fruits and vegetables.
2. Let the child write down what you need in each food group. Then together check and put down things for cleaning and other things at the grocery store, such as soap, light bulbs, and so on.
3. Look at the list together and try to think of how much money you will spend. If you save food coupons, see which ones you can use.
4. Look over the list again to see if everything is on it.
5. At the store let the child pick out some things, like which fruit, cereal, salad dressing, and so on. Show the child how to pick out what is best.
6. When you buy something by weight, let the child put it in the bag, then weigh it and think about how much it will cost.
7. Check some things for price, like one kind of peas or another one.
8. If more than one child is with you, have as many bags filled as there are children, so that each has a bag. They can put them into the shopping cart, car, or carry them home. (Suggestions: You may want to do this on the same day each week. It may be one of the things the child must do each week.)

❏ *Sense of Importance*
● **IT IS GOOD TO LEARN TO WRITE ABOUT YOUR FEELINGS AND THINGS THAT HAPPEN.**
1. Try to get the child to keep a log, journal, or diary.
2. Some ideas for this are what you did each day, favorite sports, school, and so on.
3. Write in the book every day before bedtime.
4. No one should look at it or read it…only if he or she shows it to someone and wants to share it.
5. This is a very good thing for a child to do when he or she likes to write. It also teaches the child to write better.
6. Praise the child for the time he or she spent writing and keeping it up, even if the child writes just a little a few times a week.

❏ *Self-respect*
● **HELP THE CHILD WHEN HE OR SHE FEELS BAD BECAUSE OF WHAT SOME-ONE SAID ABOUT HIM OR HER.**
1. You can help the child feel good by teaching him or her to say something like, "I like myself and, at least, I don't have to stoop to saying mean things to others". Have the child keep saying this over and over again!
2. When other children say bad things to him or her, teach the child to say, "That's what you think, but at least I don't try to hurt other people's feelings."
3. Have the child practice saying these things to you so that he or she gets used to them.
4. If the sentences here do not work for your child, make up others. He or she should be able to say something to help him or her feel better, and something to the other child who said something bad.

❏ *Approval* ❏ *Acceptance*
● **IT IS GOOD TO HAVE THE CHILD'S FRIEND BE WITH YOUR FAMILY WHEN YOU ALL DO SOMETHING TOGETHER.**
1. Pick out a few things to do that your child's friend can do with you.
2. Let your child pick a friend he or she wants to ask to be with you.
3. Before your child asks the friend, there are things that he or she should be able to tell the friend:
(1) What you will be doing;

(continued…)

(2) What time he or she should come to your house or be picked up and the time he or she will be home;

(3) How both of them should act.

4. Try to say mostly good things about the friend while you're together and afterwards.

☐ *Approval* ☐ *Sense of Power*
☐ *Sense of Importance*

● **THE CHILD SHOULD MAKE A SCRAPBOOK.**

1. Try to get the child to pick out something that he or she likes to do, and then get pictures and different "things" about it.

2. Some good items to put in scrapbooks are: cars, animals, rock stars, ball players, and so on.

3. You do not have to buy a book for this. Pages or paper can be stapled or tied together with string.

4. The child can paste the pictures and items in the scrapbook any way he or she wants.

5. Ask to see the scrapbook and praise him or her for the work. Ask questions about it. Let the child know that you like the work.

6. Talk about the good things the work shows. "You know a lot about baseball trivia!", "Your work shows you've learned a lot on your own about this."

❐ *Responsibility* ❐ *Self-respect* ❐ *Pride*

● **THE CHILD NEEDS TO HAVE GOOD HABITS KEEPING HIS OR HER BODY AND HAIR CLEAN.**

1. Make sure the child has the things needed for keeping clean.
2. Tell the child how often he or she needs to use these things and how to be able to tell on your own if they need to be used:
   - toothbrush—two times a day
   - deodorant—every morning
   - shower or bath—one time a day or when sweaty or dirty
   - hairbrush, comb—whenever hair looks messy

   (Show the child how to best brush or comb his or her hair and how it should look when it's done neat enough.)

❐ *Trust* ❐ *Acceptance*

● **WHILE THE FAMILY EATS DINNER, IT IS GOOD TO TALK ABOUT THE DAY.**

1. When everyone has their food, Mother or Father can start by telling a good thing that happened that day or what he or she liked about the day.
2. If someone else doesn't tell something good about their day, try to get the child to do this.
3. If the child still doesn't say anything, you may tell about something good in his or her day that you saw, such as he or she brought home good papers, a friend called, he or she got along with a brother or sister, and so on.
4. When a child does share something, be sure to say something good about what he or she said.
5. Try to do this every day.

❐ *Acceptance* ❐ *Self-respect*

● **THE FAMILY CAN PLAY A GAME TOGETHER.**

1. Turn off the TV and pick out a game.
2. Everyone in the family should take turns in picking out the game.
3. Pick only those games that you have or can do, such as checkers, dominos, poker, monopoly, and so on. Other games that do not cost anything are: Simon Says, Hangman, Hopscotch, Jump Rope, Tag, Red Rover, Red Light-Green Light, Paper-Scissors-Rock, "Name That Tune".
4. Plan the time to play the game, and for how long it should be played.
5. Be sure everyone knows the rules of the game, how it should be played, and how to act when playing.
6. When playing, have fun! It is not important who wins the game.

❐ *Trust* ❐ *Sense of Power*
❐ *Sense of Importance*

● **TALK WITH THE CHILD ABOUT HIS OR HER SCRAPBOOK. (Note: Make sure the child has one; if not, try to get him or her to start one.)**

1. Ask the child to tell you about the scrapbook.
2. Ask the child to tell you about something that he or she has that is special.
3. If the child is able, have him or her tell you how he or she got started in this interest, and got all the things in the scrapbook.
4. Tell the child about the things you were interested in when you were a child.
5. Help the child with the scrapbook. You can bring things for it.

❏ *Trust*

● **RELAXATION. (This is a way to take control of YOU! It helps you to find a focus, control stress, and relax.)**
(Suggestion: This can be a great "after break" idea for the entire class. It can be a real relaxer!)

1. Sit straight in your chair. Be stiff, feet flat on the floor.
2. Tighten your muscles. Starting at your toes—up through your feet. TIGHTER—up your legs to your waist. TIGHTER—your chest— shoulders—arms—make fists of your hands. TIGHTER...TIGHTER!
3. Lift your shoulders up to your ears—down— slowly—again—up—down—again.
4. Move your head as far forward as you can. Let your chin touch your chest.
5. Move your head back. Stretch those neck muscles.
6. Do numbers four and five three times.
7. Begin to relax your muscles. Start at the top of your head and slowly work your way down to the tips of your toes—SLOWLY— RELAX!— RELAX!—RELAX!—Feel your muscles go limp. Relax.
8. Sit quietly and enjoy feeling relaxed (10 seconds). (Suggest that you can do this yourself, for yourself—any time, any place, when you feel angry or upset or alone.)

❏ *Acceptance* ❏ *Self-respect*

● **PLAY A GAME TOGETHER.**

1. Turn off the TV and pick out a game.
2. Everyone in the family should take turns in picking out the game.
3. Pick only those games that you have or can do, such as checkers, dominos, poker, monopoly, and so on. Other games that do not cost anything are: Simon Says, Hangman, Hopscotch, Jump Rope, Tag, Red Rover, Red Light-Green Light, Paper-Scissors-Rock, "Name That Tune".
4. Plan the time to play the game, and for how long it should be played.
5. Be sure everyone knows the rules of the game, how it should be played, and how to act when playing.
6. When playing, have fun! It is not important who wins the game.

❏ *Trust* ❏ *Sense of Power*
❏ *Sense of Importance*

● **TALK WITH THE CHILD ABOUT HIS OR HER SCRAPBOOK. (Note: Make sure the child has one; if not, try to get him or her to start one.)**

1. Ask the child to tell you about the scrapbook.
2. Ask the child to tell you about something that he or she has that is special.
3. If the child is able, have him or her tell you how he or she got started in this interest, and got all the things in the scrapbook.
4. Tell the child about the things you were interested in when you were a child.
5. Help the child with the scrapbook. You can bring things for it.

Level 12 Characteristics

- Emotional intensities; highs and lows
- Sense of humor and fair play
- Trying to find and define self
- Critical of own appearance
- Self-preoccupied
- Difficulty accepting praise
- Less participation in family activities
- More critical of parents
- Personal interests specialize on a variety of topics (sports, spirituality, proving themselves with peers)
- Emphasis on Best Friends
- Either hate or love school
- Restless
- Horseplays
- Learning to work in groups
- Wants privacy
- Wants to be like everybody else (peer influence and trends are important)
- Movie-going
- Telephoning and gossiping
- Forms relationships with other adults outside the family as role models (i.e., teacher, coach, aunt, etc.)
- Strong need for parental approval; needs to have opinion taken seriously versus need for growing independence
- Self-made authorities
- Gender-related interests are more exaggerated:
  a) Girls romantically interested in boys and may expend more energy and attention on heterosexual activities;
  b) Boys like things with wheels...cars, skateboards, etc.
- Sexual development issues:
  a) Sexual interest or activity may begin at this age—masturbation, wet dreams, etc.; interest or activity continues to increase;
  b) Physical development and changes (height, weight, pubic hair, breasts);
  c) Peer pressure to be involved in or discuss sexual activities.
- Experimentation with sex, drugs and alcohol may occur

Level 12 Information

Self-esteem is a feeling.
If you have HIGH self-esteem...
> You make good friends!
> You care about yourself and other people;
> You are responsible;
> You enjoy learning;
> You are proud of what you do;
> You can handle failure;
> You can share feelings.

HIGH self-esteem is having a GOOD feeling about yourself, your place in the family, your school, and your world.

THINGS TO REMEMBER:
- Children will not talk to you very much at this age.
- Look the child IN THE EYE when you TALK or LISTEN.
- It is important to KEEP TALKING to him or her...even if you think you aren't getting anywhere.
- Ask questions...Answer your own questions...Just KEEP TALKING!
- HUMOR is important...be "funny" and let him or her be "funny".
- Use the child's name.
- If you like something the child is doing or wearing, tell them EXACTLY what you like. It shows you aren't just saying it and that you care.
- If the child tells you about something he or she did well...PRAISE him or her.
- When you first see the child after school or work and the child has done something wrong and you are upset, try to say at least 2 GOOD THINGS to him or her BEFORE you talk about any bad things.
- Children take things in their life SERIOUSLY. You should, too. This shows RESPECT for the child.
- FIND A REASON TO SAY EACH OF THESE PHRASES ONCE A DAY:
  I like to be with you.
  I like your good work.

DON'T GIVE UP!
— If the child does not want to do the activity with you the way you want him or her to...try again tomorrow.
— Keep trying. This is the way you **SHOW** the child that you mean what you say. A child needs to **TRUST** in order to share with you or listen to you.
— **HOW** you say something is sometimes more important than **WHAT** you say.

You may be doing MOST of these things already as part of the way you care for children and run your home. By doing these things in the way they are written, you will be helping the child's self-esteem **plus** your own self-esteem.

When you can help somebody feel good... you feel good!

"I" messages let the child know exactly what you want, why you want it, and how you want it. The child does not have to GUESS what you want or how you feel. This is a way of setting LIMITS. Some examples are:
- **"I** feel very upset when you throw your clothes on the floor. Clothes cost money... **I** work hard for my money and **I** want you to have nice clothes to wear."
- **"I** do not want you to carry those two full glasses of milk at one time. **I** am afraid they will spill."

The BASE program is about helping children have HIGH self-esteem. It is a group of things to do and share with a child. These things are short, simple and positive. They should be done everyday when possible.

REMEMBER:
If any of these things do not agree with the way you believe or your religion (example: dancing), do not do it.

Level 12 Human Awareness

Here are some things for you to talk about with your teenager. It means a lot for you to let the teenager know that you want to talk about these things.

What you should say when the teenager asks you something:

Always answer even if it seems that he or she is asking in order to shock you. You build self-esteem when you answer. If you *do not* tell what he or she wants to know, the teen learns: 1. not to ask you things; or, 2. that he or she is not "old" enough or "good" enough.

When you can, both parents should share in teaching about sex. Be sure to talk about diseases that you can get from someone when you have sex with them, such as herpes and AIDS. When both parents are a part of this, the teen sees sex education as a family thing.

Telling teens about sex will not make them think more about it or over-stimulate them.

Don't be afraid to say, "I don't know". You should then try to find the answer. There are books about this that the teen can understand. First read the book by yourself so that you know what is in it. Then read it with the teen.

Be sure you know what your own values are...how you think about things...what is right or wrong.

It is okay to talk together about different ways of thinking; ways that may be different from the way you may feel.

Keep your sense of humor.

Don't try to be perfect. No one is always right.

When you talk about something that is hard for you, it is okay to say, "This makes me uncomfortable, but because I love you, it's something we need to talk about". The teenager might be just as uncomfortable or as embarrassed as you are!

Some questions may shock you, but you should be sure to answer them. If not, the teenager may ask someone else and he or she may not have your values or know the facts. When the teenager asks shocking questions about contraceptives or oral sex, he or she is letting you know that he or she trusts you.

You may say, "I see that your body is starting to change. If you have any questions or if there is something you're wondering about, I'm here." Let the teen know that it is your job, because you are the parent, to help and guide him or her to understand questions about life, his or her body, sex, and making good choices in what you do and say. "We all think about sex, some thoughts are good and some are bad, but this is normal and okay. If you want to talk about it, I am here. Come to me any time."

Tell the teen what is "normal"...
1. Changes in the body are normal, but everyone's body doesn't change at the same time. Boys and girls grow at different speeds, some slower and some faster. In some, hormones may be starting to "take over your body" so wet dreams are normal, irregular periods are normal, and so on. *(continued...)*

Level 12 Human Awareness

2. Tell the teen that there are many ways to show affection, love and caring. Intercourse is only one of the many ways. Other ways can be hugging and kissing. Talking together can also be intimate.

3. It is important to teach the teen to make good choices in what he or she does and says. Help the teenager to learn what will happen when you do some things. Teaching how to make a good choice is better for your teenager than making demands and threats. You cannot be with your teenager every minute.

4. Let the teen know that some people, when they are dating, have sex so that they can "use" someone, and that can really hurt a boy or girl.

It is good for the teenager to be close to others of his or her own sex that are about the same age.

The teenager will have changes in his or her body. These changes may make him or her feel excited, frightened, as well as embarrassed.

The teenager's mood may change from one way to another often. This is because of changes in hormones (growing fast or sometimes slower). The teen may cry "for no reason" or sulk. Teenagers are often critical of their parents and embarrassed by them. They are very concerned about what others think and think a lot about how their body looks.

Teenagers need and want you to answer their questions and show that you care when you do this.

If the teenager talks about things that make you think he or she may have been sexually abused, tell a health care professional.

When the teenager asks questions that you don't have answers for, ask your family doctor, clinic, or health department.

REMEMBER:
If anything written here is against your religious or moral beliefs, don't do it!

Level 12 Teacher Information

(To be used with **C** Exercises)

Your cooperation with these exercises is VERY IMPORTANT.

As you know, success or failure in school is directly tied to self-esteem. The intelligent child with low self-esteem will do poorly in school...the average child with HIGH self-esteem will generally be successful.

It's also true that low self-esteem gets in the way of good performance and that bad performance reinforces low self-esteem.

This exercise can be done with the child alone in the beginning. Within a week or so, you might want to share it with the entire class. This exercise works very well as a "calmer downer" after recess, or break.

This is a way of trying to show a little **extra special attention** to a child who is very much in need of POSITIVE strokes.

Look for the POSITIVE and PRAISE it. Use the child's name when giving PRAISE. Be specific with the PRAISE.

Your support is appreciated!

❏ Trust ❏ Acceptance
- **IT IS GOOD FOR THE FAMILY TO EAT TOGETHER WHEN THEY CAN AND TALK ABOUT A CURRENT EVENT OR SOMETHING THAT IS HAPPENING NOW.**
1. Try to pick a meal when most or all of the family are eating together. Let everyone have a chance to talk.
2. Let someone pick a current event and try to get each one to talk about it.
3. If no one has anything to talk about, you should be ready with something that the children would like to talk about.
4. During the day you may say to the teen, "This may be something you would like to talk about at dinner tonight".
5. It is okay for each one to feel differently about what you are talking about. Each should feel free to say what they think, and know that the others will let them talk.

❏ Acceptance ❏ Responsibility
- **EVERYONE IN THE FAMILY MUST HELP WITH THE JOBS TO BE DONE AROUND THE HOUSE.**
1. Talk about what the jobs are and how they should be done.
2. Plan who will do each job. Some jobs are not as nice to do as others. Everyone should do the same number of nice, and not so nice jobs.
3. Make sure everyone knows that "we all pitch in as a family".
4. Make a list of the teenager's jobs so that he or she can check off when the job is done.
5. Make sure that he or she knows how *you* want the job done. You may want to show how the job can best be done.
6. When a job is done, or done well, praise the teen, give a reward, or let him or her work for something special.

❏ Responsibility
- **LET THE TEENAGER KNOW THAT HIS OR HER HOMEWORK IS IMPORTANT TO YOU.**
1. Talk about the work as something that is good.
2. Ask the teen to share one thing he or she learned at school today.
3. It is very important to *listen* and see how he or she thinks about things. Do not correct or lecture, or say he or she is wrong.

❏ Approval ❏ Trust ❏ Acceptance
- **IT IS IMPORTANT TO TOUCH THE TEENAGER IN THE RIGHT WAY.**
1. Even when a child gets older, it is important for the teen to be touched in some way.
2. Touch the teen in a way that he or she feels comfortable or feels it is okay.
3. You may want to hug or give a pat on the back when you feel close to him or her, when you're glad to see him or her, or when he or she does a good job.
4. The teen may want to sit next to you so he or she will feel close, maybe when watching TV.
5. If the teenager does not like to be touched...don't push it. Take it slow.

❏ Trust
- **TALK ABOUT FAMILIES.**
1. Meal time may be a good time to talk.
2. Things you want the teenager to know:
   A. Families may be made up in different ways. There may be only a father or a mother. A family may have grandparents, aunts, cousins, and so on. A family may be a stepfather or stepmother with children, so there are stepbrothers and stepsisters.
   B. No one kind of family is best. All kinds can be okay.
   C. Every family has different rules, and that's okay. No one set of rules is best or right. Everyone in the family must live by their family rules.
3. Ways to help the teenager when he or she says something about the different ones in the family.
   A. Everyone in the family can be different and have different things happen in their life. This is okay.
   B. You should not say that one child is better than the other in any way. They may be different, but don't let them get the feeling that he or she is better or not as good.

❏ Trust ❏ Acceptance
- **TELL THE TEENAGER SOMETHING ABOUT YOURSELF. WHEN YOU *SHARE*, YOU ARE TELLING HIM OR HER THAT YOU *TRUST*!**
1. Tell the teen if you had a funny, sad, or interesting thing happen to you today. (You may want to do this at dinner or during a quiet time.)

(continued...)

2. When you are talking, do not think he or she will answer your questions; they often do not at this age.
3. When some good or bad things of life happen to the teen, you may want to tell about when that happened to you, such as going on a first date, first time you drove a car, failing a test, winning a prize, having to write a theme, and so on.
4. When the time is right, tell things that happened to you as a teenager, if the teen likes to hear them and is not bored. Be sure you are not making it a "put-down" for him or her by *bragging* that you did something better.

Optional (if needed):
❐ *Sense of Power* ❐ *Responsibility*
❐ *Self-respect*
❐ *Pride* ❐ *Respect for Others*

● **YOU SHOULD TRY HARD TO HELP HIM OR HER MAKE ONE FRIEND.**
1. Talk with the teen about how he or she feels about making friends. Is it hard, easy, fun, or does he or she like to make new friends?
2. Ask what kind of friends the teen liked before."What did you like about him or her?"
3. Have the teen think about the people he or she knows, and how it makes him or her feel.
   A. Keep the friends that make you feel good when you're with them.
   B. You have to be a friend, and that helps you to make a new friend.
   C. Stay away from the ones that make you feel bad or get you into a problem.
4. Let the teen know that we all often feel shy when making friends.
5. Let the teen know that some things about him or her are good and "other kids will like you when they get to know you". (Talk about the good things by saying: "I *think* you are honest" or "I *think* you can be trusted" or "I *think* that you are fun to be with")
6. Talk about things the teen can do or talk about with new friends, such as going to movies, talk about sports, homework, and so on.
7. Some activities the teen may want to do with a new friend:
   1. Try to learn to do something new.
   2. Learn to cook.
   3. Take exercise classes.
   4. Learn to use a camera.
   5. Work to earn money to buy new records, clothes, or something special you want.
   6. Volunteer to help a children's group.

❐ *Responsibility* ❐ *Respect for Others*
● **THERE SHOULD BE SOME RULES FOR USING THE TELEPHONE IN YOUR HOME.**
1. Talk with the teen about the rules for using the telephone.
2. Be sure the teen knows how you feel about how long he or she talks on the phone, calls after a special time at night, making long distance calls, and so on.
3. Tell the teen what will happen if these rules are broken. (i.e., no phone calls for one or two days, or not going to a "favorite" activity, and so on.)
4. There may be a time when the teen cannot keep the rules. If there is a good reason, try to understand and work it out together.

❐ *Approval* ❐ *Acceptance* ❐ *Respect for Others*
● **ASK YOUR TEEN'S FRIEND TO BE WITH YOUR FAMILY WHEN YOU DO SOMETHING.**
1. Pick an activity that needs or could use his or her friend's help.
2. Let the teen pick out a friend, and ask him or her to come to your home.
3. Show the teen that you are interested in his or her friend by sometimes asking, "How's Bobby?"
4. When you plan activities, think of the teen and if he or she would like to have someone his or her own age with you when you do this.
5. When you can, have the teen do a job during the family activity. His or her friend could help with it.

❐ *Responsibility* ❐ *Sense of Importance*
❐ *Respect for Others*
● **IT IS GOOD FOR THE TEEN TO GET TO KNOW OTHER ADULTS AND "LOOK UP TO THEM".**
1. Sometimes have an adult that isn't part of the family be with you for an activity.
2. You may ask him or her to dinner, a picnic, and so on.
3. You may ask a minister, grandmother, neighbor, or family friend.

❏ *Trust* ❏ *Sense of Power* ❏ *Responsibility*
❏ *Self-respect* ❏ *Respect for Others*

● *PEER PRESSURE!* **OTHER TEENAGERS OFTEN TRY TO GET HIM OR HER TO DO THINGS, SOME GOOD AND SOME BAD.**

1. Talk together about friends wanting the teen to do something. Think if these are good, bad, or in-between things to do.
2. Talk together about how the teen may want to do something so he or she can be part of a group. Friends may ask the teen to do something, and he or she wants the friends to like him or her.
3. Help the teen think if he or she wants, or doesn't want to do what friends say.
   a. Would I do this on my own, or do it to please my friend?
   b. Is it something that is wrong to do?
   c. How will I feel if I do it? Will I feel guilty that I did the wrong thing?
4. How would you handle it if your friends want you to:
   a. skip school?
   b. take drugs or drink?
   c. destroy someone else's property?
   d. "pick-on" another person (be a bully)?
5. Talk about how the teen can get out of being someplace or doing something that is not right.
   a. Together plan a "code". It can be one word or a few words that means he or she wants you to come and get him or her. "Just called to say "Hello"! ("Hello" may be the *code* word.)
   b. The friends should not know about the "code". This way the teen can use it when he or she needs to get away from the friends.
6. Have the teen say some of the things over and over in front of you so that it will be easy to say it to others, such as "I don't do drugs". Say family rules, such as "I can't do that, I have to be home in ten minutes".
7. Ask the teenager to list "rights and wrongs". If he or she can't, help him or her with the list.
8. Try to get the teen to lead or get his or her friends to do things that are okay. Think before you act!

❏ *Sense of Power* ❏ *Self-respect* ❏ *Pride*
● **SHARE THIS WITH YOUR TEENAGER:**
1. You may know the difference between things that are right and things that are wrong to do.

Sometimes a friend or group can try to get you to do something you really don't want to do or something that you don't think is right to do, but you don't want them to think that you are afraid or a "chicken". When friends want you to do something you know is bad for you, or something that could get you into trouble...try saying this:
- "No thanks, I don't do drugs!" or
- "No thanks, I don't drink!" or
- "No thanks, I don't want to trash that house!"
- "You may like the way it makes you feel, but I don't like the way it makes me feel now or later, so I don't want to do it!"

Have the teen try saying this to you so that he or she can hear how it sounds. Then have the teen practice saying this to himself or herself over and over again...so that when put on the spot by a "friend", the teen will know what to say and what it feels like to say it.

❏ *Self-respect* ❏ *Pride* ❏ *Sense of Importance*
● **TEACH THE TEENAGER TO SAY THIS: "I AM A WORTHWHIILE PERSON...I LIKE ME."**
1. Help the teen think about what is good about himself or herself, what people can see in him or her, and what he or she has good on the inside. How nice the teen is to other people. How considerate, respectful, caring he or she is. How the teen keeps clean and neat. How reliable he or she is, and so on.
2. Talk to the teen about things you think are good and special about him or her. "You must be proud of yourself. I would be if I knew I could do that."

❏ *Sense of Power*
● **IT IS GOOD TO LEARN TO WRITE ABOUT YOUR FEELINGS AND THINGS THAT HAPPEN IN YOUR LIFE.**
1. Give the teen the items he or she needs to have a diary, journal, log, or write letters (pen and paper or notebook).
2. If the teen has a diary or log, do not look at it. It is important for the teen to feel that he or she can write anything and no one will see it, unless he or she wants to share it.

❏ *Responsibility*

● **LET THE TEENAGER KNOW THAT HIS OR HER HOMEWORK IS IMPORTANT TO YOU.**

1. Talk about the work as something that is good.
2. Ask the teen to share one thing he or she learned at school today.
3. It is very important to *listen* and see how he or she thinks about things. Do not correct or lecture, or say he or she is wrong.

❏ *Approval* ❏ *Trust* ❏ *Acceptance*

● **IT IS IMPORTANT TO TOUCH THE TEENAGER IN THE RIGHT WAY.**

1. Even when a child gets older, it is important for the teen to be touched in some way.
2. Touch the teen in a way that he or she feels comfortable or feels it is okay.
3. You may want to hug or give a pat on the back when you feel close to him or her, when you're glad to see him or her, or when he or she does a good job.
4. The teen may want to sit next to you so he or she will feel close, maybe when watching TV.
5. If the teenager does not like to be touched...don't push it. Take it slow.

❏ *Trust*

● **TALK ABOUT FAMILIES.**

1. Meal time may be a good time to talk.
2. Things you want the teenager to know:
   A. Families may be made up in different ways. There may be only a father or a mother. A family may have grandparents, aunts, cousins, and so on. A family may be a stepfather or stepmother with children, so there are stepbrothers and stepsisters.
   B. No one kind of family is best. All kinds can be okay.
   C. Every family has different rules, and that's okay. No one set of rules is best or right. Everyone in the family must live by their family rules.
3. Ways to help the teenager when he or she says something about the different ones in the family.
   A. Everyone in the family can be different and have different things happen in their life. This is okay.
   B. You should not say that one child is better than the other in any way. They may be different, but don't let them get the feeling that he or she is better or not as good.

❏ *Trust* ❏ *Acceptance*

● **TELL THE TEENAGER SOMETHING ABOUT YOURSELF. WHEN YOU *SHARE*, YOU ARE TELLING HIM OR HER THAT YOU *TRUST*!**

1. Tell the teen if you had a funny, sad, or interesting thing happen to you today. (You may want to do this at dinner or during a quiet time.)
2. When you are talking, do not think he or she will answer your questions; they often do not at this age.
3. When some good or bad things of life happen to the teen, you may want to tell about when that happened to you, such as going on a first date, first time you drove a car, failing a test, winning a prize, having to write a theme, and so on.
4. When the time is right, tell things that happened to you as a teenager, if the teen likes to hear them and is not bored. Be sure you are not making it a "put-down" for him or her by *bragging* that you did something better.

❏ *Trust* ❏ *Sense of Power* ❏ *Responsibility*
❏ *Self-respect* ❏ *Respect for Others*

● ***PEER PRESSURE!* OTHER TEENAGERS OFTEN TRY TO GET HIM OR HER TO DO THINGS, SOME GOOD AND SOME BAD.**

1. Talk together about friends wanting the teen to do something. Think if these are good, bad, or in-between things to do.
2. Talk together about how the teen may want to do something so he or she can be part of a group. Friends may ask the teen to do something, and he or she wants the friends to like him or her.
3. Help the teen think if he or she wants, or doesn't want to do what friends say.
   a. Would I do this on my own, or do it to please my friend?
   b. Is it something that is wrong to do?
   c. How will I feel if I do it? Will I feel guilty that I did the wrong thing?
4. How would you handle it if your friends want you to:
   a. skip school?
   b. take drugs or drink?
   c. destroy someone else's property?
   d. "pick-on" another person (be a bully)?

(continued...)

5. Talk about how the teen can get out of being someplace or doing something that is not right.
   a. Together plan a "code". It can be one word or a few words that means he or she wants you to come and get him or her. "Just called to say "Hello"! ("Hello" may be the *code* word.)
   b. The friends should not know about the "code". This way the teen can use it when he or she needs to get away from the friends.
6. Have the teen say some of the things over and over in front of you so that it will be easy to say it to others, such as "I don't do drugs". Say family rules, such as "I can't do that, I have to be home in ten minutes".
7. Ask the teenager to list "rights and wrongs". If he or she can't, help him or her with the list.
8. Try to get the teen to lead or get his or her friends to do things that are okay. Think before you act!

**READ CAREFULLY BEFORE YOU DO
THIS EXERCISE WITH THE CHILD
OR CLASS.**
☐ *Trust*

● **SELF-CONTROL EXERCISES. A WAY TO
RELAX AND GET RID OF STRESS
(2 minutes).**

1. Get comfortable. Put both feet on the floor, sit
straight. Have your hands rest on your knees
and eyes closed.

2. Let all the tension out of your body—relax.
Make a picture in your mind of a place that's
very peaceful, quiet, beautiful. It may be by a
stream or in a meadow, or other places.

3. Now put yourself in that peaceful picture. See
the colors. Hear the sounds, the birds, the wind
through the trees. Smell the air. How fresh and
clean it is! Feel the warmth of the sun.

4. This is your own private place. You can go there
at any time, from any place, whenever you want
to "just get away".

5. You feel happy there—at peace, in control of
yourself. You feel strong and good about
yourself. Just being there gives you new energy.

6. Just relax. Count to 10 in your mind and then
open your eyes.

❏ *Approval* ❏ *Trust* ❏ *Acceptance*

● **IT IS IMPORTANT TO TOUCH THE TEENAGER IN THE RIGHT WAY.**

1. Even when a child gets older, it is important for the teen to be touched in some way.
2. Touch the teen in a way that he or she feels comfortable or feels it is okay.
3. You may want to hug or give a pat on the back when you feel close to him or her, when you're glad to see him or her, or when he or she does a good job.
4. The teen may want to sit next to you so he or she will feel close, maybe when watching TV.
5. If the teenager does not like to be touched...don't push it. Take it slow.

❏ *Trust* ❏ *Acceptance*

● **TELL THE TEENAGER SOMETHING ABOUT YOURSELF. WHEN YOU *SHARE*, YOU ARE TELLING HIM OR HER THAT YOU *TRUST*!**

1. Tell the teen if you had a funny, sad, or interesting thing happen to you today. (You may want to do this at dinner or during a quiet time.)
2. When you are talking, do not think he or she will answer your questions; they often do not at this age.
3. When some good or bad things of life happen to the teen, you may want to tell about when that happened to you, such as going on a first date, first time you drove a car, failing a test, winning a prize, having to write a theme, and so on.
4. When the time is right, tell things that happened to you as a teenager, if the teen likes to hear them and is not bored. Be sure you are not making it a "put-down" for him or her by *bragging* that you did something better.

❏ *Self-respect* ❏ *Pride* ❏ *Sense of Importance*

● **TEACH THE TEENAGER TO SAY THIS: "I AM A WORTHWHILE PERSON...I LIKE ME."**

1. Help the teen think about what is good about himself or herself, what people can see in him or her, and what he or she has good on the inside. How nice the teen is to other people. How considerate, respectful, caring he or she is. How the teen keeps clean and neat. How reliable he or she is, and so on.
2. Talk to the teen about things you think are good and special about him or her. "You must be proud of yourself. I would be if I knew I could do that."

9th grade

Level 13 Characteristics

- Emotional intensities; highs and lows
- Sense of humor and fair play
- Trying to find and define self
- Critical of own appearance
- Self-preoccupied; fears failure and loss of face
- Difficulty accepting praise
- Less participation in family activities
- More critical of parents, yet needs parental approval
- Personal interests focus in a few areas
- Emphasis on best friends
- Either hates or loves school
- Restless and horseplays
- Learning to work in groups
- Wants privacy
- Wants to be like everybody else (peer influence and trends are important)
- Movie-going, telephoning and gossiping
- Forms relationships with other adults outside the family as role models (i.e., teacher, coach, aunt, etc.)
- Self-made authorities
- Gender-related interests are more exaggerated:
  a) Girls romantically interested in boys and may expend more energy and attention on heterosexual activities;
  b) Boys like things with wheels...cars, skateboards, etc.
- Sexual development issues:
  a) Boys are becoming more prone to try to satisfy sexual drive;
  b) Girls sexual interest or activity continues to increase;
  c) Peer pressure to be involved in or discuss sexual activities.
- Self-acceptance of own positive qualities
- Needs adult encouragement for the development of self
- The competitive world has arrived
- Values being tested while standing up to own convictions in the face of peers
- May be experimenting with sex, drugs, and alcohol
- Grade placement (i.e., schools 1st grade to 8th grade, 9th grade to 12th grade vs. 7th grade to 9th grade) makes a big difference in self-confidence and esteem.

Level 13 Information

Self-esteem is a feeling.
If you have HIGH self-esteem...
>   You make good friends!
>   You care about yourself and other people;
>   You are responsible;
>   You enjoy learning;
>   You are proud of what you do;
>   You can handle failure;
>   You can share feelings.

HIGH self-esteem is having a GOOD feeling about yourself, your place in the family, your school, and your world.

THINGS TO REMEMBER:
- Teens will not talk to you very much at this age.
- Look the teen IN THE EYE when you TALK or LISTEN.
- It is important to KEEP TALKING to him or her...even if you think you aren't getting anywhere.
- Ask questions...Answer your own questions...Just KEEP TALKING!
- HUMOR is important...be "funny" and let him or her be "funny".
- Use the teen's name.
- If you like something the teen is doing or wearing, tell them EXACTLY what you like. It shows you aren't just saying it and that you care.
- If the teen tells you about something he or she did well...PRAISE him or her.
- When you first see the teen after school or work and the child has done something wrong and you are upset, try to say at least 2 GOOD THINGS to him or her BEFORE you talk about any bad things.
- Teens take things in their life SERIOUSLY. You should, too. This shows RESPECT for the child.
- FIND A REASON TO SAY EACH OF THESE PHRASES ONCE A DAY:
  I like to be with you.
  I like your good work.

DON'T GIVE UP!
— If the teen does not want to do the activity with you the way you want him or her to...try again tomorrow.
— Keep trying. This is the way you **SHOW** the teen that you mean what you say. A teen needs to **TRUST** in order to share with you or listen to you.
— **HOW** you say something is sometimes more important than **WHAT** you say.

You may be doing MOST of these things already as part of the way you care for teenagers and run your home. By doing these things in the way they are written, you will be helping the teen's self-esteem **plus** your own self-esteem.

When you can help somebody feel good... you feel good!

"I" messages let the teen know exactly what you want, why you want it, and how you want it. The teen does not have to GUESS what you want or how you feel. This is a way of setting LIMITS. Some examples are:
- "**I** feel very upset when you throw your clothes on the floor. Clothes cost money... **I** work hard for my money and **I** want you to have nice clothes to wear."

The BASE program is about helping teens have HIGH self-esteem. It is a group of things to do and share with a teen. These things are short, simple and positive. They should be done everyday when possible.

REMEMBER:
If any of these things do not agree with the way you believe or your religion (example: dancing), do not do it.

Level 13 Human Awareness

What you should say when the teenager asks you something:

Always answer even if it seems that he or she is asking in order to shock you. You build self-esteem when you answer. If you *do not* tell what he or she wants to know, the teen learns: 1. not to ask you things; or, 2. that he or she is not "old" enough or "good" enough.

When you can, both parents should share in teaching about sex. Be sure to talk about diseases that you can get from someone when you have sex with them, such as herpes and AIDS. When both parents are a part of this, the teen sees sex education as a family thing.

Telling teens about sex will not make them think more about it or over-stimulate them.

Don't be afraid to say, "I don't know". You should then try to find the answer. There are books about this that the teen can understand. First read the book by yourself so that you know what is in it. Then read it *with* the teen.

Be sure you know what your own values are…how you think about things…what is right or wrong.

It is okay to talk together about different ways of thinking; ways that may be different from the way you may feel.

Let the teen know that it is normal and okay for there to be changes in his or her body.

Keep your sense of humor.

Tell the teen what is "normal"…

1. Changes in the body are normal, but everyone's body doesn't change at the same time. Boys and girls grow at different speeds, some slower and some faster. In some, hormones may be starting to "take over your body" so wet dreams are normal, irregular periods are normal, and so on.

2. Tell the teen that there are many ways to show affection, love and caring. Intercourse is only one of the many ways. Other ways can be hugging and kissing. Talking together can also be intimate.

3. It is important to teach the teen to make good choices in what he or she does and says. Help the teenager to learn what will happen when you do some things. Teaching how to make a good choice is better for your teenager than making demands and threats. You cannot be with your teenager every minute.

4. Let the teen know that some people, when they are dating, have sex so that they can "use" someone, and that can really hurt a boy or girl.

The teenager will have changes in his or her body. These changes may make him or her feel excited, frightened, as well as embarrassed.

The teenager's mood may change from one way to another often. This is because of changes in hormones (growing fast or sometimes slower). The teen may cry "for no reason", or sulk. Teenagers are often critical of their parents and

(continued…)

Level 13 Human Awareness

embarrassed by them. They are very concerned about what others think and think a lot about how their body looks.

Teenagers need and want you to answer their questions and show that you care when you do this.

Teenagers want to know about the right way to act...birth control, love and relationships. There are many kinds of RELATIONSHIPS:
1. Someone you know
2. Friend
3. Good friend
4. Boy friend or girl friend
5. Person you become engaged to
6. Husband or wife

During some quiet time, try to get the teenager to ask questions. Let him or her know that, "This is my job as a parent. I need to explain and help you understand the big questions of life...to help you understand your body...to help you learn how to make good choices and decisions. We all think about sex, some thoughts are good and some are bad, but this is normal and okay. If you want to talk about it, I am here. Come to me anytime."

If the teenager talks about things that make you think he or she may have been sexually abused, tell a health care professional.

When the teenager asks questions that you don't have answers for, ask your family doctor, clinic, or health department.

REMEMBER:
If anything written here is against your religious or moral beliefs, don't do it!

Level 13 Teacher Information

(To be used with **C** Exercises)

Your cooperation with these exercises is VERY IMPORTANT.

As you know, success or failure in school is directly tied to self-esteem. The intelligent child with low self-esteem will do poorly in school...the average child with HIGH self-esteem will generally be successful.

It's also true that low self-esteem gets in the way of good performance and that bad performance reinforces low self-esteem.

This exercise can be done with the child alone in the beginning. Within a week or so, you might want to share it with the entire class. This exercise works very well as a "calmer downer" after recess, or break.

This is a way of trying to show a little **extra special attention** to a child who is very much in need of POSITIVE strokes.

Look for the POSITIVE and PRAISE it.
Use the child's name when giving PRAISE.
Be specific with the PRAISE.

Your support is appreciated!

❒ *Trust* ❒ *Acceptance*

● **TELL THE TEENAGER SOMETHING ABOUT YOURSELF. WHEN YOU *SHARE*, YOU ARE TELLING HIM OR HER THAT YOU *TRUST*!**

1. Tell the teen if you had a funny, sad, or interesting thing happen to you today. (You may want to do this at dinner or during a quiet time.)
2. When you are talking, do not think he or she will answer your questions; they often do not at this age.
3. When some good or bad things of life happen to the teen, you may want to tell about when that happened to you, such as going on a first date, first time you drove a car, failing a test, winning a prize, having to write a theme, and so on.
4. When the time is right, tell things that happened to you as a teenager, if the teen likes to hear them and is not bored. Be sure you are not making it a "put-down" for him or her by *bragging* that you did something better.

Optional (if needed):
❒ *Sense of Power* ❒ *Responsibility*
❒ *Self-respect*
❒ *Pride* ❒ *Respect for Others*

● **YOU SHOULD TRY HARD TO HELP HIM OR HER MAKE ONE FRIEND.**

1. Talk with the teen about how he or she feels about making friends. Is it hard, easy, fun, or does he or she like to make new friends?
2. Ask what kind of friends the teen liked before."What did you like about him or her?"
3. Have the teen think about the people he or she knows, and how it makes him or her feel.
   A. Keep the friends that make you feel good when you're with them.
   B. You have to be a friend, and that helps you to make a new friend.
   C. Stay away from the ones that make you feel bad or get you into a problem.
4. Let the teen know that we all often feel shy when making friends.
5. Let the teen know that some things about him or her are good and "other kids will like you when they get to know you". (Talk about the good things by saying: "I *think* you are honest" or "I *think* you can be trusted" or "I *think* that you are fun to be with")
6. Talk about things the teen can do or talk about with new friends, such as going to movies, talk about sports, homework, and so on.
7. Some activities the teen may want to do

with a new friend:
1. Try to learn to do something new.
2. Learn to cook.
3. Take exercise classes.
4. Learn to use a camera.
5. Work to earn money to buy new records, clothes, or something special you want.
6. Volunteer to help a children's group.

❒ *Responsibility* ❒ *Respect for Others*

● **THERE SHOULD BE SOME RULES FOR USING THE TELEPHONE IN YOUR HOME.**

1. Talk with the teen about the rules for using the telephone.
2. Be sure the teen knows how you feel about how long he or she talks on the phone, calls after a special time at night, making long distance calls, and so on.
3. Tell the teen what will happen if these rules are broken. (i.e., no phone calls for one or two days, or not going to a "favorite" activity, and so on.)
4. There may be a time when the teen cannot keep the rules. If there is a good reason, try to understand and work it out together.

❒ *Approval* ❒ *Acceptance* ❒ *Respect for Others*

● **ASK YOUR TEEN'S FRIEND TO BE WITH YOUR FAMILY WHEN YOU DO SOMETHING.**

1. Pick an activity that needs or could use his or her friend's help.
2. Let the teen pick out a friend, and ask him or her to come to your home.
3. Show the teen that you are interested in his or her friend by sometimes asking, "How's Bobby?"
4. When you plan activities, think of the teen and if he or she would like to have someone his or her own age with you when you do this.
5. When you can, have the teen do a job during the family activity. His or her friend could help with it.

❒ *Responsibility* ❒ *Sense of Importance* ❒ *Respect for Others*

● **IT IS GOOD FOR THE TEEN TO GET TO KNOW OTHER ADULTS AND "LOOK UP TO THEM".**

1. Sometimes have an adult that isn't part of the family be with you for an activity.
2. You may ask him or her to dinner, a picnic, and so on.

(continued...)

3. You may ask a minister, grandmother, neighbor, or family friend.

❏ *Trust* ❏ *Sense of Power* ❏ *Responsibility*
❏ *Self-respect* ❏ *Respect for Others*

● *PEER PRESSURE!* **OTHER TEENAGERS OFTEN TRY TO GET HIM OR HER TO DO THINGS, SOME GOOD AND SOME BAD.**

1. Talk together about friends wanting the teen to do something. Think if these are good, bad, or in-between things to do.
2. Talk together about how the teen may want to do something so he or she can be part of a group. Friends may ask the teen to do something, and he or she wants the friends to like him or her.
3. Help the teen think if he or she wants, or doesn't want to do what friends say.
   a. Would I do this on my own, or do it to please my friend?
   b. Is it something that is wrong to do?
   c. How will I feel if I do it? Will I feel guilty that I did the wrong thing?
4. How would you handle it if your friends want you to:
   a. skip school?
   b. take drugs or drink?
   c. destroy someone else's property?
   d. "pick-on" another person (be a bully)?
5. Talk about how the teen can get out of being someplace or doing something that is not right.
   a. Together plan a "code". It can be one word or a few words that means he or she wants you to come and get him or her. "Just called to say "Hello"! ("Hello" may be the *code* word.)
   b. The friends should not know about the "code". This way the teen can use it when he or she needs to get away from the friends.
6. Have the teen say some of the things over and over in front of you so that it will be easy to say it to others, such as "I don't do drugs". Say family rules, such as "I can't do that, I have to be home in ten minutes".
7. Ask the teenager to list "rights and wrongs". If he or she can't, help him or her with the list.
8. Try to get the teen to lead or get his or her friends to do things that are okay. Think before you act!

❏ *Sense of Power* ❏ *Self-respect* ❏ *Pride*

● **SHARE THIS WITH YOUR TEENAGER:**

1. You may know the difference between things that are right and things that are wrong to do.

Sometimes a friend or group can try to get you to do something you really don't want to do or something that you don't think is right to do, but you don't want them to think that you are afraid or a "chicken". When friends want you to do something you know is bad for you, or something that could get you into trouble...try saying this:
• "No thanks, I don't do drugs!" or
• "No thanks, I don't drink!" or
• "No thanks, I don't want to trash that house!"
• "You may like the way it makes you feel, but I don't like the way it makes me feel now or later, so I don't want to do it!"
Have the teen try saying this to you so that he or she can hear how it sounds. Then have the teen practice saying this to himself or herself over and over again...so that when put on the spot by a "friend", the teen will know what to say and what it feels like to say it.

❏ *Trust* ❏ *Acceptance*

● **IT IS GOOD FOR THE FAMILY TO EAT TOGETHER WHEN THEY CAN AND TALK ABOUT A CURRENT EVENT OR SOMETHING THAT IS HAPPENING NOW.**

1. Try to pick a meal when most or all of the family are eating together. Let everyone have a chance to talk.
2. Let someone pick a current event and try to get each one to talk about it.
3. If no one has anything to talk about, you should be ready with something that the children would like to talk about.
4. During the day you may say to the teen, "This may be something you would like to talk about at dinner tonight".
5. It is okay for each one to feel differently about what you are talking about. Each should feel free to say what they think, and know that the others will let them talk.

❏ *Acceptance* ❏ *Responsibility*

● **EVERYONE IN THE FAMILY MUST HELP WITH THE JOBS TO BE DONE AROUND THE HOUSE.**

1. Talk about what the jobs are and how they should be done.
2. Plan who will do each job. Some jobs are not as nice to do as others. Everyone should do the same number of nice, and not so nice jobs.
3. Make sure everyone knows that "we all pitch in as a family".

(continued...)

4. Make a list of the teenager's jobs so that he or she can check off when the job is done.

5. Make sure that he or she knows how *you* want the job done. You may want to show how the job can best be done.

6. When a job is done, or done well, praise the teen, give a reward, or let him or her work for something special.

❏ *Responsibility*

● **LET THE TEENAGER KNOW THAT HIS OR HER HOMEWORK IS IMPORTANT TO YOU.**

1. Talk about the work as something that is good.

2. Ask the teen to share one thing he or she learned at school today.

3. It is very important to *listen* and see how he or she thinks about things. Do not correct or lecture, or say he or she is wrong.

❏ *Approval* ❏ *Trust* ❏ *Acceptance*

● **IT IS IMPORTANT TO TOUCH THE TEENAGER IN THE RIGHT WAY.**

1. Even when a child gets older, it is important for the teen to be touched in some way.

2. Touch the teen in a way that he or she feels comfortable or feels it is okay.

3. You may want to hug or give a pat on the back when you feel close to him or her, when you're glad to see him or her, or when he or she does a good job.

4. The teen may want to sit next to you so he or she will feel close, maybe when watching TV.

5. If the teenager does not like to be touched...don't push it. Take it slow.

❏ *Trust*

● **TALK ABOUT FAMILIES.**

1. Meal time may be a good time to talk.

2. Things you want the teenager to know:
   A. Families may be made up in different ways. There may be only a father or a mother. A family may have grandparents, aunts, cousins, and so on. A family may be a stepfather or stepmother with children, so there are stepbrothers and stepsisters.
   B. No one kind of family is best. All kinds can be okay.
   C. Every family has different rules, and that's okay. No one set of rules is best or right. Everyone in the family must live by their family rules.

3. Ways to help the teenager when he or she says something about the different ones in the family.
   A. Everyone in the family can be different and have different things happen in their life. This is okay.
   B. You should not say that one child is better than the other in any way. They may be different, but don't let them get the feeling that he or she is better or not as good.

❏ *Self-respect* ❏ *Pride* ❏ *Sense of Importance*

● **TEACH THE TEENAGER TO SAY THIS: "I AM A WORTHWHILE PERSON...I LIKE ME."**

1. Help the teen think about what is good about himself or herself, what people can see in him or her, and what he or she has good on the inside. How nice the teen is to other people. How considerate, respectful, caring he or she is. How the teen keeps clean and neat. How reliable he or she is, and so on.

2. Talk to the teen about things you think are good and special about him or her. "You must be proud of yourself. I would be if I knew I could do that."

❏ *Sense of Power*

● **IT IS GOOD TO LEARN TO WRITE ABOUT YOUR FEELINGS AND THINGS THAT HAPPEN IN YOUR LIFE.**

1. Give the teen the items he or she needs to have a diary, journal, log, or write letters (pen and paper or notebook).

2. If the teen has a diary or log, do not look at it. It is important for the teen to feel that he or she can write anything and no one will see it, unless he or she wants to share it.

Optional:
❏ *Approval* ❏ *Responsibility*

● **IF POSSIBLE, WORK OUT AN ALLOWANCE FOR THE CHILD AND TALK ABOUT WHAT SHOULD BE DONE WITH THIS MONEY.**

1. You could plan with the teen a way for him or her to earn money. This could be given to him or her for doing jobs, and so on.

2. Plan with the teen what will be done with the money. Some of it could be saved, some spent on things he or she really needs, some for fun, and so on.

❏ *Responsibility*
- **LET THE TEENAGER KNOW THAT HIS OR HER HOMEWORK IS IMPORTANT TO YOU.**
1. Talk about the work as something that is good.
2. Ask the teen to share one thing he or she learned at school today.
3. It is very important to *listen* and see how he or she thinks about things. Do not correct or lecture, or say he or she is wrong.

❏ *Trust* ❏ *Acceptance*
- **TELL THE TEENAGER SOMETHING ABOUT YOURSELF. WHEN YOU *SHARE*, YOU ARE TELLING HIM OR HER THAT YOU *TRUST*!**
1. Tell the teen if you had a funny, sad, or interesting thing happen to you today. (You may want to do this at dinner or during a quiet time.)
2. When you are talking, do not think he or she will answer your questions; they often do not at this age.
3. When some good or bad things of life happen to the teen, you may want to tell about when that happened to you, such as going on a first date, first time you drove a car, failing a test, winning a prize, having to write a theme, and so on.
4. When the time is right, tell things that happened to you as a teenager, if the teen likes to hear them and is not bored. Be sure you are not making it a "put-down" for him or her by *bragging* that you did something better.

❏ *Approval* ❏ *Acceptance*
- **TRY TO FIND SOMETHING THAT YOU BOTH LIKE TO DO AND TALK ABOUT.**
1. Ask the teen what he or she is interested in, or likes to do, such as running, sewing, music, cars, animals, clothes, and so on.
2. Try to get the teen to tell you what he or she knows about the subject or interest.
3. Let the teen know that "you learned from him or her".
4. Thank the teen for telling you about his or her interests...for sharing!

❏ *Trust* ❏ *Sense of Power* ❏ *Responsibility*
❏ *Self-respect* ❏ *Respect for Others*
- ***PEER PRESSURE!* OTHER TEENAGERS OFTEN TRY TO GET HIM OR HER TO DO THINGS, SOME GOOD AND SOME BAD.**
1. Talk together about friends wanting the teen to do something. Think if these are good, bad, or in-between things to do.
2. Talk together about how the teen may want to do something so he or she can be part of a group. Friends may ask the teen to do something, and he or she wants the friends to like him or her.
3. Help the teen think if he or she wants, or doesn't want to do what friends say.
   a. Would I do this on my own, or do it to please my friend?
   b. Is it something that is wrong to do?
   c. How will I feel if I do it? Will I feel guilty that I did the wrong thing?
4. How would you handle it if your friends want you to:
   a. skip school?
   b. take drugs or drink?
   c. destroy someone else's property?
   d. "pick-on" another person (be a bully)?
5. Talk about how the teen can get out of being someplace or doing something that is not right.
   a. Together plan a "code". It can be one word or a few words that means he or she wants you to come and get him or her. "Just called to say "Hello"! ("Hello" may be the *code* word.)
   b. The friends should not know about the "code". This way the teen can use it when he or she needs to get away from the friends.
6. Have the teen say some of the things over and over in front of you so that it will be easy to say it to others, such as "I don't do drugs". Say family rules, such as "I can't do that, I have to be home in ten minutes".
7. Ask the teenager to list "rights and wrongs". If he or she can't, help him or her with the list.
8. Try to get the teen to lead or get his or her friends to do things that are okay. Think before you act!

READ CAREFULLY BEFORE YOU DO THIS EXERCISE WITH THE TEENAGER OR CLASS.

❐ *Trust*

● **SELF-CONTROL EXERCISES. A WAY TO RELAX AND GET RID OF STRESS.**

1. Get comfortable. Relax. Close your eyes or look into your lap.
2. Picture yourself in a place where you feel safe and happy. It should be a beautiful, comfortable place. This place is all your own.
3. Think about the way you are breathing. Feel the air move in through your nose, now out through your mouth.
4. In 1-2-3, take in more and more air. Out 1-2-3, let it all out, every drop.
5. Do number 4 three more times.
6. Listen to the quiet while you breathe slowly.
7. Think only about the air and how in and out breathing gives you LIFE.
8. Relax and enjoy the quiet way you feel.
9. You know that the place where you go to relax belongs only to you. You can be there any time, from any place, no one has to know you're there in your mind. When you're upset, mad, or frightened, you can take yourself "away from it all". You can relax a little and get control of what is happening and your situation.

❏ *Approval* ❏ *Acceptance*

● **TRY TO FIND SOMETHING THAT YOU BOTH LIKE TO DO AND TALK ABOUT.**

1. Ask the teen what he or she is interested in, or likes to do, such as running, sewing, music, cars, animals, clothes, and so on.
2. Try to get the teen to tell you what he or she knows about the subject or interest.
3. Let the teen know that "you learned from him or her".
4. Thank the teen for telling you about his or her interests...for sharing!

❏ *Approval* ❏ *Trust* ❏ *Acceptance*

● **IT IS IMPORTANT TO TOUCH THE TEENAGER IN THE RIGHT WAY.**

1. Even when a child gets older, it is important for the teen to be touched in some way.
2. Touch the teen in a way that he or she feels comfortable or feels it is okay.
3. You may want to hug or give a pat on the back when you feel close to him or her, when you're glad to see him or her, or when he or she does a good job.
4. The teen may want to sit next to you so he or she will feel close, maybe when watching TV.
5. If the teenager does not like to be touched...don't push it. Take it slow.

❏ *Self-respect* ❏ *Pride* ❏ *Sense of Importance*

● **TEACH THE TEENAGER TO SAY THIS: "I AM A WORTHWHILE PERSON...I LIKE ME."**

1. Help the teen think about what is good about himself or herself, what people can see in him or her, and what he or she has good on the inside. How nice the teen is to other people. How considerate, respectful, caring he or she is. How the teen keeps clean and neat. How reliable he or she is, and so on.
2. Talk to the teen about things you think are good and special about him or her. "You must be proud of yourself. I would be if I knew I could do that."

10th grade

Level 14 Characteristics

- Can be serious
- Need for privacy
- Guarded about self
- More discriminating about what he or she shares with whom
- Need for independence—needs to be needed
- Learning to combine efforts to reach short term objectives
- Separating from family
- Unhappiness is apparent if forced to do anything
- Group friendships
- Congregates
- Group activities common
- May be negative toward anything that does not provide instant gratification
- Learning to accept responsibility for his or her own behavior
- Enjoys spectator sports
- Peer trends guide behavior (fads, usually different from adult norms)
- Questions authority
- Growing consciousness of physical self-image (appearance, grooming, etc.)
- Educational turning point
- Possible experimentation with sex, drugs, and alcohol

Level 14 Information

Self-esteem is a feeling.
If you have HIGH self-esteem...
> You make good friends!
> You care about yourself and other people;
> You are responsible;
> You enjoy learning;
> You are proud of what you do;
> You can handle failure;
> You can share feelings.

HIGH self-esteem is having a GOOD feeling about yourself, your place in the family, your school, and your world.

THINGS TO REMEMBER:
- Teens will not talk to you very much at this age.
- Look the teen IN THE EYE when you TALK or LISTEN.
- It is important to KEEP TALKING to him or her...even if you think you aren't getting anywhere.
- Ask questions...Answer your own questions...Just KEEP TALKING!
- HUMOR is important...be "funny" and let him or her be "funny".
- Use the teen's name.
- If you like something the teen is doing or wearing, tell them EXACTLY what you like. It shows you aren't just saying it and that you care.
- If the teen tells you about something he or she did well...PRAISE him or her.
- When you first see the teen after school or work and the child has done something wrong and you are upset, try to say at least 2 GOOD THINGS to him or her BEFORE you talk about any bad things.
- Teens take things in their life SERIOUSLY. You should, too. This shows RESPECT for the child.
- FIND A REASON TO SAY EACH OF THESE PHRASES ONCE A DAY:
  I like to be with you.
  I like your good work.

DON'T GIVE UP!
— If the teen does not want to do the activity with you the way you want him or her to...try again tomorrow.
— Keep trying. This is the way you **SHOW** the teen that you mean what you say. A teen needs to **TRUST** in order to share with you or listen to you.
— **HOW** you say something is sometimes more important than **WHAT** you say.

You may be doing MOST of these things already as part of the way you care for teenagers and run your home. By doing these things in the way they are written, you will be helping the teen's self-esteem **plus** your own self-esteem.

When you can help somebody feel good... you feel good!

"I" messages let the teen know exactly what you want, why you want it, and how you want it. The teen does not have to GUESS what you want or how you feel. This is a way of setting LIMITS. Some examples are:
- "**I** feel very upset when you throw your clothes on the floor. Clothes cost money... **I** work hard for my money and **I** want you to have nice clothes to wear."

The BASE program is about helping teens have HIGH self-esteem. It is a group of things to do and share with a teen. These things are short, simple and positive. They should be done everyday when possible.

REMEMBER:
If any of these things do not agree with the way you believe or your religion (example: dancing), do not do it.

Level 14 Human Awareness

Here are some things for you to talk about with your teenager. It means a lot for you to let the teenager know that you want to talk about these things.

When you can, both parents should share in teaching about sex. Be sure to talk about diseases that you can get from someone when you have sex with them, such as herpes and AIDS. When both parents are a part of this, the teen sees sex education as a family thing.

Telling teens about sex will not make them think more about it or over-stimulate them.

Don't be afraid to say, "I don't know". Together you should try to find the answer. There are many books at the library.

Be sure you know what your own values are...how you think about things...what is right or wrong.

It is okay to talk together about different ways of thinking; ways that may be different from the way you may feel.

Let the teen know that it is normal and okay for there to be changes in his or her body.

Keep your sense of humor.

Don't try to be perfect. No one is always right.

When you talk about sex, don't talk to the boys alone or girls alone. Boys and girls need to know how the other's body works. Boys will be living around women all their lives. They need to know about ovulation, contraception (how to keep from getting pregnant or sexual diseases),

and menstruation (the period or "curse"). Girls also need to know how the man's body works. You want to be sure they learn that sex is something that the family can talk about.

When you talk about something that is hard for you, it is okay to say, "This makes me uncomfortable, but because I love you, it's something we need to talk about". The teenager might be just as uncomfortable or as embarrassed as you are!

Tell the teen what is "normal"...

1. Changes in the body are normal, but everyone's body doesn't change at the same time. Boys and girls grow at different speeds, some slower and some faster. In some, hormones may be starting to "take over your body" so wet dreams are normal, irregular periods are normal, and so on.

2. Tell the teen that there are many ways to show affection, love and caring. Intercourse is only one of the many ways. Other ways can be hugging and kissing. Talking together can also be intimate.

3. It is important to teach the teen to make good choices in what he or she does and says. Help the teenager to learn what will happen when you do some things. Teaching how to make a good choice is better for your teenager than making demands and threats. You cannot be with your teenager every minute.

4. Let the teen know that some people, when they are dating, have sex so that they can "use" someone, and that can really hurt a boy or girl. *(continued...)*

Level 14 Human Awareness

Teenagers need and want you to answer their questions and show that you care when you do this.

Teenagers want to know about the right way to act...birth control, love and relationships. There are many kinds of RELATIONSHIPS:

1. Someone you know
2. Friend
3. Good friend
4. Boy friend or girl friend
5. Person you become engaged to
6. Husband or wife

During some quiet time, try to get the teenager to ask questions. Let him or her know that, "This is my job as a parent. I need to explain and help you understand the big questions of life...to help you understand your body...to help you learn how to make good choices and decisions. We all think about sex, some thoughts are good and some are bad, but this is normal and okay. If you want to talk about it, I am here. Come to me anytime."

If the teenager talks about things that make you think he or she may have been sexually abused, tell a health care professional.

When the teenager asks questions that you don't have answers for, ask your family doctor, clinic, or health department.

REMEMBER:
If anything written here is against your religious or moral beliefs, don't do it!

Level 14 Teacher Information

(To be used with **C** Exercises)

Your cooperation with these exercises is VERY IMPORTANT.

As you know, success or failure in school is directly tied to self-esteem. The intelligent child with low self-esteem will do poorly in school...the average child with HIGH self-esteem will generally be successful.

It's also true that low self-esteem gets in the way of good performance and that bad performance reinforces low self-esteem.

This exercise can be done with the teen alone in the beginning. Within a week or so, you might want to share it with the entire class. This exercise works very well as a "calmer downer".

This is a way of trying to show a little extra special attention to a teen who is very much in need of POSITIVE strokes.

Look for the POSITIVE and PRAISE it.
Use the teen's name when giving PRAISE.
Be specific with the PRAISE.

Talk with the teenager about social, moral, and political issues or things that happen. You do not have to agree with or think the same way as the teen does, but he or she should know that he or she has a right to think in his or her own way. You should both give your ideas when talking.

By this time, most teens have fairly set opinions, ideas, thoughts on many things that have to do with their lives, such as social and political issues and positions, lifestyles, moral issues, and so on. It is important for parents, teachers and others to know the teen's opinions, thoughts, and feelings in these areas. It is important that you NOT set yourself up as a judge and jury to decide if the teen is right or wrong. Try to say something good to the teen about his or her ideas whenever possible. Try to talk so that you can get a better understanding of the way the teen thinks when you don't agree.

Your support is appreciated!

☐ *Sense of Power* ☐ *Responsibility*
☐ *Self-respect* ☐ *Respect for Others*
☐ *Flexibility*

- **YOU NEED TO SET UP HOUSE RULES AND THE WAY YOU THINK THE TEENAGER SHOULD ACT. Be sure to talk about *why* you have these rules and *how* they should be followed.**
1. List the family's rules.
2. Ask if the teen has any questions about the rules.
3. Ask the teen if he or she can put down any other special rules for different seasons, holidays, and so on.
4. When you can, try to use the teenager's ideas or rules.
5. If the teen's suggestions won't work, try to tell him or her why you cannot use them. Be sure to ask for other suggestions. Keep doing this.
6. Talk about special times when some of the rules can be changed for that one time, such as prom night.

☐ *Approval* ☐ *Trust*
☐ *Acceptance* ☐ *Sense of Importance*

- **TAKE TIME TO TALK WITH THE TEENAGER ABOUT MANY THINGS.**
1. You can start to talk about something he or she is interested in, such as things happening now in the news, sports, neighborhood, school, and so on.
2. Ask what the teen thinks about something— his or her ideas, feelings, the way he or she might handle something.
3. Try to get the teenager to give ideas by saying something that shows you like what he or she says, such as "You have a good idea", or "I would not have thought of that, that's great!"
4. Ask questions about the teen's ideas. "How would you change situations or things?", "How do you think other kids feel about the situation?"
5. Talk about how you feel and think about something without making the teenager feel you don't like the way he or she thinks (don't be critical). You don't have to agree, but you should respect others' opinions or thoughts.
6. Look at the teenager when you're talking.
7. You can start talking with him or her any time you think of something. It may be while eating, watching TV, listening to music, riding in the car, and so on.

8. You may want to show the teen that it is okay for you not to feel the same way he or she feels by giving a friendly touch on his or her arm or shoulder.
9. End your talk in a good way. "I really like your idea" or "What you said gives me something to think about."

☐ *Trust*

- **YOU AND THE TEENAGER SHOULD TALK ABOUT FAMILIES.**
1. Meal time may be a good time to talk.
2. Things you want the teenager to know:
   A. Families may be made up in different ways. There may be only a father or a mother. A family may have grandparents, aunts, cousins, and so on. A family may be a stepfather or stepmother with children, so there are stepbrothers and stepsisters.
   B. No one kind of family is best. All kinds can be okay.
   C. Every family has different rules, and that's okay. No one set of rules is best or right. Everyone in the family must live by their family rules.
3. Ways to help the teenager when he or she says something about the different ones in the family.
   A. Everyone in the family can be different and have different things happen in their life. This is okay.
   B. You should not say that one child is better than the other in any way. They may be different, but don't let them get the feeling that he or she is better or not as good.

☐ *Trust* ☐ *Sense of Power* ☐ *Responsibility*
☐ *Self-respect* ☐ *Respect for Others*

- ***PEER PRESSURE!* OTHER TEENAGERS OFTEN TRY TO GET HIM OR HER TO DO THINGS, SOME GOOD AND SOME BAD.**
1. Talk together about friends wanting the teen to do something. Think if these are good, bad, or in-between things to do.
2. Talk together about how the teen may want to do something so he or she can be part of a group. Friends may ask the teen to do something, and he or she wants the friends to like him or her.
3. Help the teen think if he or she wants, or doesn't want to do what friends say.
   a. Would I do this on my own, or do it to please my friend?

(continued...)

b. Is it something that is wrong to do?

c. How will I feel if I do it? Will I feel guilty that I did the wrong thing?

4. How would you handle it if your friends want you to:

   a. skip school?

   b. take drugs or drink?

   c. destroy someone else's property?

   d. "pick-on" another person (be a bully)?

5. Talk about how the teen can get out of being someplace or doing something that is not right.

   a. Together plan a "code". It can be one word or a few words that means he or she wants you to come and get him or her. "Just called to say "Hello"! ("Hello" may be the *code* word.)

   b. The friends should not know about the "code". This way the teen can use it when he or she needs to get away from the friends.

6. Have the teen say some of the things over and over in front of you so that it will be easy to say it to others, such as "I don't do drugs". Say family rules, such as "I can't do that, I have to be home in ten minutes".

7. Ask the teenager to list "rights and wrongs". If he or she can't, help him or her with the list.

8. Try to get the teen to lead or get his or her friends to do things that are okay. Think before you act!

❐ Sense of Power ❐ Self-respect ❐ Pride

● **SHARE THIS WITH YOUR TEENAGER:**

1. You may know the difference between things that are right and things that are wrong to do. Sometimes a friend or group can try to get you to do something you really don't want to do or something that you don't think is right to do, but you don't want them to think that you are afraid or a "chicken". When friends want you to do something you know is bad for you, or something that could get you into trouble...try saying this:

   • "No thanks, I don't do drugs!" or

   • "No thanks, I don't drink!" or

   • "No thanks, I don't want to trash that house!"

   • "You may like the way it makes you feel, but I don't like the way it makes me feel now or later, so I don't want to do it!"

Have the teen try saying this to you so that he or she can hear how it sounds. Then have the teen practice saying this to himself or herself over and over again...so that when put on the spot by a "friend", the teen will know what to say and what it feels like to say it.

❐ Acceptance ❐ Flexibility
❐ Sense of Importance

● **HELP THE TEENAGER TO PLAN FOR HIS OR HER FUTURE.**

1. Start to talk to the teen about what he or she would like to do (such as jobs, school), where to live, live with someone, marriage, and so on.

2. Wait until you think the teen is able to tell you honestly what goals and dreams he or she has. Then talk about what he or she must do to get ready for this.

3. Together, think of the steps that must be taken; how much and what kind of education, what money is needed and how to get it, how to get to where you need to be, what skills are needed, and so on.

❐ Approval ❐ Sense of Power ❐ Responsibility
❐ Self-respect ❐ Pride ❐ Sense of Importance

● **HELP THE TEENAGER MAKE A PLAN FOR USING THE MONEY HE OR SHE EARNS.**

1. Talk with the teen and together think about what he or she needs and what he or she wants to spend the money on, and how much to *save*.

2. Help the teen to think what is the most important thing to use the money for, the next important thing, and so on.

3. Tell the teen that *gross* pay is *all* the money you get, and *net* pay is how much you have left after you use some for the job; such as car fare, uniforms, taxes, and so on.

4. Help the teen plan a *budget*; how much to spend on needs, wants, entertainment, and savings.

5. If possible, go to the bank with the teen to open a checking and/or a savings account.

6. Show the teen how to write a check, mark it in the book, and balance the check book. You should help the teen until you are sure he or she can do it alone.

❑ *Sense of Power* ❑ *Responsibility*
❑ *Respect for Others* ❑ *Flexibility*

● **TRY TO HAVE FAMILY MEETINGS TO TALK ABOUT THINGS THAT ARE NOT RIGHT, GIVE IDEAS FOR THE FAMILY, THINK WHAT TO DO ABOUT A PROBLEM, OR GIVE PRAISE, AND SO ON.**

1. Have the meetings every week or when someone (any family member) wants a meeting.
2. Each parent should be at the meeting and help to keep it in order.
3. Make some rules:
   a. When can a meeting be called? Anyone in the family should be able to call a meeting.
   b. How long should a meeting last?
   c. Everyone in the family should be at the meeting.
   d. Make rules about the way you should talk, such as no "put-downs", no name calling, and so on.
4. Before the meeting, the parent should meet with each person who has a problem to bring up:
   a. Talk about the problem;
   b. Help the teenager find the right way to present the problem to the group; and
   c. Have the teenager practice the way he or she will talk about the problem with the group.
5. Parents should make sure that everyone has a chance to tell what he or she feels. Then the family should work on a way to help what is wrong, or agree that it cannot be made better.
6. If necessary, tell different ones in the family to do some things to help with a problem.
7. *Always end the meeting with a good feeling. This is very important.*

❒ *Approval* ❒ *Trust*
❒ *Acceptance* ❒ *Sense of Importance*

● **TAKE TIME TO TALK WITH THE TEENAGER ABOUT MANY THINGS.**

1. You can start to talk about something he or she is interested in, such as things happening now in the news, sports, neighborhood, school, and so on.

2. Ask what the teen thinks about something— his or her ideas, feelings, the way he or she might handle something.

3. Try to get the teenager to give ideas by saying something that shows you like what he or she says, such as "You have a good idea", or "I would not have thought of that, that's great!"

4. Ask questions about the teen's ideas. "How would you change situations or things?", "How do you think other kids feel about the situation?"

5. Talk about how you feel and think about something without making the teenager feel you don't like the way he or she thinks (don't be critical). You don't have to agree, but you should respect others' opinions or thoughts.

6. Look at the teenager when you're talking.

7. You can start talking with him or her any time you think of something. It may be while eating, watching TV, listening to music, riding in the car, and so on.

8. You may want to show the teen that it is okay for you not to feel the same way he or she feels by giving a friendly touch on his or her arm or shoulder.

9. End your talk in a good way. "I really like your idea.", or "What you said gives me something to think about."

❒ *Trust* ❒ *Sense of Power* ❒ *Responsibility*
❒ *Self-respect* ❒ *Respect for Others*

● *PEER PRESSURE!* **OTHER TEENAGERS OFTEN TRY TO GET HIM OR HER TO DO THINGS, SOME GOOD AND SOME BAD.**

1. Talk together about friends wanting the teen to do something. Think if these are good, bad, or in-between things to do.

2. Talk together about how the teen may want to do something so he or she can be part of a group. Friends may ask the teen to do something, and he or she wants the friends to like him or her.

3. Help the teen think if he or she wants, or doesn't want to do what friends say.
   a. Would I do this on my own, or do it to please my friend?
   b. Is it something that is wrong to do?
   c. How will I feel if I do it? Will I feel guilty that I did the wrong thing?

4. How would you handle it if your friends want you to:
   a. skip school?
   b. take drugs or drink?
   c. destroy someone else's property?
   d. "pick-on" another person (be a bully)?

5. Talk about how the teen can get out of being someplace or doing something that is not right.
   a. Together plan a "code". It can be one word or a few words that means he or she wants you to come and get him or her. "Just called to say "Hello"! ("Hello" may be the *code* word.)
   b. The friends should not know about the "code". This way the teen can use it when he or she needs to get away from the friends.

6. Have the teen say some of the things over and over in front of you so that it will be easy to say it to others, such as "I don't do drugs". Say family rules, such as "I can't do that, I have to be home in ten minutes".

7. Ask the teenager to list "rights and wrongs". If he or she can't, help him or her with the list.

8. Try to get the teen to lead or get his or her friends to do things that are okay. Think before you act!

❒ *Acceptance* ❒ *Flexibility*
❒ *Sense of Importance*

● **HELP THE TEENAGER TO PLAN FOR HIS OR HER FUTURE.**

1. Start to talk to the teen about what he or she would like to do (such as jobs, school), where to live, live with someone, marriage, and so on.

2. Wait until you think the teen is able to tell you honestly what goals and dreams he or she has. Then talk about what he or she must do to get ready for this.

3. Together, think of the steps that must be taken; how much and what kind of education, what money is needed and how to get it, how to get to where you need to be, what skills are needed, and so on.

READ CAREFULLY BEFORE YOU DO THIS EXERCISE WITH THE TEENAGER OR CLASS.

☐ *Trust*

● **RELAXATION/STRESS REDUCING EXERCISE—GAINING CONTROL OF YOURSELF.**

1. Close your eyes or look down into your lap.
2. Relax—Relax!
3. Breathe in through your nose/out through your mouth—listen to the air move in and out.
4. Picture yourself in the place where you feel the most safe and peaceful—a beautiful place— a calm place. You're a part of the place— keep breathing—deeper—deeper.
5. Focus on yourself.
6. As you let the air out—let out any anger or frustration or fear—with every breath—the GOOD flows in—the BAD flows out. The POSITIVE moves in—the NEGATIVE moves out!
7. Listen to the air. Feel it surrounding you.
8. Relax in your own special place. In through your nose/out through your mouth.
9. Get control of yourself/hold on to the POSITIVE!
10. When you're ready—open your eyes.
    (Tell the teenager or class that is something you can do at any time—wherever you may be— when you are angry, frustrated, depressed, misunderstood, sad or upset.)

❏ *Approval* ❏ *Trust*
❏ *Acceptance* ❏ *Sense of Importance*

● **TAKE TIME TO TALK WITH THE
TEENAGER ABOUT MANY THINGS.**

1. You can start to talk about something he or she is interested in, such as things happening now in the news, sports, neighborhood, school, and so on.

2. Ask what the teen things about something— his or her ideas, feelings, the way he or she might handle something.

3. Try to get the teenager to give ideas by saying something that shows you like what he or she says, such as "You have a good idea" or "I would not have thought of that, that's great!"

4. Ask questions about the teen's ideas. "How would you change situations or things?", "How do you think other kids feel about the situation?"

5. Talk about how you feel and think about something without making the teenager feel you don't like the way he or she thinks (don't be critical). You don't have to agree, but you should respect others' opinions or thoughts.

6. Look at the teenager when you're talking.

7. You can start talking with him or her any time you think of something. It may be while eating, watching TV, listening to music, riding in the car, and so on.

8. You may want to show the teen that it is okay for you not to feel the same way he or she feels by giving a friendly touch on his or her arm or shoulder.

9. End your talk in a good way. "I really like your idea." or "What you said gives me something to think about."

11th-12th grade

Level 15 Characteristics

- Young people on this level tend to cover up feelings
- Maturing, coping skills
- More sociable and outgoing
- Learning to manage and handle independent living skills (i.e., management of money, time, etc.)
- Spends less time with family
- More in control of impulses
- More willing to discuss issues
- Feels equal or superior to parents, older siblings, other adults
- Unrealistic expectation about adult life (freedom...get-away mentality)
- Inaccurate perception of own power to make his or her dreams come true
- Experimentation with sex, drugs, and alcohol may occur

Level 15 Information

Self-esteem is a feeling.
If you have HIGH self-esteem...
> You make good friends!
> You care about yourself and other people;
> You are responsible;
> You enjoy learning;
> You are proud of what you do;
> You can handle failure;
> You can share feelings.

HIGH self-esteem is having a GOOD feeling about yourself, your place in the family, your school, and your world.

THINGS TO REMEMBER:
- Teens will not talk to you very much at this age.
- Look the teen IN THE EYE when you TALK or LISTEN.
- It is important to KEEP TALKING to him or her...even if you think you aren't getting anywhere.
- Ask questions...Answer your own questions...Just KEEP TALKING!
- HUMOR is important...be "funny" and let him or her be "funny".
- Use the teen's name.
- If you like something the teen is doing or wearing, tell them EXACTLY what you like. It shows you aren't just saying it and that you care.
- If the teen tells you about something he or she did well...PRAISE him or her.
- When you first see the teen after school or work and the child has done something wrong and you are upset, try to say at least 2 GOOD THINGS to him or her BEFORE you talk about any bad things.
- Teens take things in their life SERIOUSLY. You should, too. This shows RESPECT for the child.
- FIND A REASON TO SAY EACH OF THESE PHRASES ONCE A DAY:
  I like to be with you.
  I like your good work.

DON'T GIVE UP!
— If the teen does not want to do the activity with you the way you want him or her to...try again tomorrow.
— Keep trying. This is the way you **SHOW** the teen that you mean what you say. A teen needs to **TRUST** in order to share with you or listen to you.
— **HOW** you say something is sometimes more important than **WHAT** you say.

You may be doing MOST of these things already as part of the way you care for teenagers and run your home. By doing these things in the way they are written, you will be helping the teen's self-esteem **plus** your own self-esteem.

When you can help somebody feel good... you feel good!

"I" messages let the teen know exactly what you want, why you want it, and how you want it. The teen does not have to GUESS what you want or how you feel. This is a way of setting LIMITS. Some examples are:
- "**I** feel very upset when you throw your clothes on the floor. Clothes cost money... **I** work hard for my money and **I** want you to have nice clothes to wear."

The BASE program is about helping teens have HIGH self-esteem. It is a group of things to do and share with a teen. These things are short, simple and positive. They should be done everyday when possible.

REMEMBER:
If any of these things do not agree with the way you believe or your religion (example: dancing), do not do it.

Level 15 Human Awareness

Here are some things for you to talk about with your teenager. It means a lot for you to let the teenager know that you want to talk about these things.

BOTH PARENTS SHOULD PARTICIPATE. When possible, both parents should share the responsibility for sex education. Men have expected most sex education to be done by the mother. When both parents participate, the teenager sees sex education as a family affair.

Be sure to talk about diseases that you can get from someone when you have sex with them, such as herpes and AIDS.

Don't be afraid to say, "I don't know". Together you should try to find an answer. There are many books at the library.

Be sure you know what your own values are...how you think about things...what is right or wrong.

It is okay to talk together about different ways of thinking; ways that may be different from the way you may feel.

Let the teen know that you like and want to be asked questions and will answer them.

Keep your sense of humor.

Don't try to be perfect. No one is always right.

If you feel that you did not give a good answer to the teenager, you may want to say something later on to him or her. "I'm sorry that I did not give you a good answer before. I would like to talk about it now", and so on.

Tell the teen what is "normal"...
1. Tell the teen that there are many ways to show affection, love and caring. Intercourse is only one of the many ways. Other ways can be hugging and kissing. Talking together can also be intimate.
2. It is important to teach the teen to make good choices in what he or she does and says. Help the teenager to learn what will happen when you do some things. Teaching how to make a good choice is better for your teenager than making demands and threats. You cannot be with your teenager every minute.
3. Let the teen know that some people, when they are dating, have sex so that they can "use" someone, and that can really hurt a boy or girl.

Teenagers need and want you to answer their questions and show that you care when you do this.

Teenagers want to know about the right way to act...birth control, love and relationships. There are many kinds of RELATIONSHIPS:
1. Someone you know
2. Friend
3. Good friend
4. Boy friend or girl friend
5. Person you become engaged to
6. Husband or wife

(continued...)

Level 15 Human Awareness

During some quiet time, try to get the teenager to ask questions. Let him or her know that, "This is my job as a parent. I need to explain and help you understand the big questions of life...to help you understand your body...to help you learn how to make good choices and decisions. We all think about sex, some thoughts are good and some are bad, but this is normal and okay. If you want to talk about it, I am here. Come to me anytime."

If the teenager talks about things that make you think he or she may have been sexually abused, tell a health care professional.

When the teenager asks questions that you don't have answers for, ask your family doctor, clinic, or health department.

REMEMBER:
If anything written here is against your religious or moral beliefs, don't do it!

Level 15 Teacher Information

(To be used with **C** Exercises)

Your cooperation with these exercises is VERY IMPORTANT.

As you know, success or failure in school is directly tied to self-esteem. The intelligent child with low self-esteem will do poorly in school...the average child with HIGH self-esteem will generally be successful.

It's also true that low self-esteem gets in the way of good performance and that bad performance reinforces low self-esteem.

This exercise can be done with the teen alone in the beginning. Within a week or so, you might want to share it with the entire class. This exercise works very well as a "calmer downer".

This is a way of trying to show a little extra special attention to a teen who is very much in need of POSITIVE strokes.

Look for the POSITIVE and PRAISE it.
Use the teen's name when giving PRAISE.
Be specific with the PRAISE.

Talk with the teenager about social, moral, and political issues or things that happen. You do not have to agree with or think the same way as the teen does, but he or she should know that he or she has a right to think in his or her own way. You should both give your ideas when talking.

By this time, most teens have fairly set opinions, ideas, thoughts on many things that have to do with their lives, such as social and political issues and positions, lifestyles, moral issues, and so on. It is important for parents, teachers and others to know the teen's opinions, thoughts, and feelings in these areas. It is important that you NOT set yourself up as a judge and jury to decide if the teen is right or wrong. Try to say something good to the teen about his or her ideas whenever possible. Try to talk so that you can get a better understanding of the way the teen thinks when you don't agree.

Your support is appreciated!

❏ *Sense of Power* ❏ *Responsibility*
❏ *Self-respect* ❏ *Respect for Others*
❏ *Flexibility*

● **YOU NEED TO SET UP HOUSE RULES AND THE WAY YOU THINK THE TEENAGER SHOULD ACT. Be sure to talk about *why* you have these rules and *how* they should be followed.**

1. List the family's rules.
2. Ask if the teen has any questions about the rules.
3. Ask the teen if he or she can put down any other special rules for different seasons, holidays, and so on.
4. When you can, try to use the teenager's ideas or rules.
5. If the teen's suggestions won't work, try to tell him or her why you cannot use them. Be sure to ask for other suggestions. Keep doing this.
6. Talk about special times when some of the rules can be changed for that one time, such as prom night.

❏ *Trust*

● **TALK ABOUT FAMILIES.**

1. Meal time may be a good time to talk.
2. Things you want the teenager to know:
   A. Families may be made up in different ways. There may be only a father or a mother. A family may have grandparents, aunts, cousins, and so on. A family may be a stepfather or stepmother with children, so there are stepbrothers and stepsisters.
   B. No one kind of family is best. All kinds can be okay.
   C. Every family has different rules, and that's okay. No one set of rules is best or right. Everyone in the family must live by their family rules.
3. Ways to help the teenager when he or she says something about the different ones in the family.
   A. Everyone in the family can be different and have different things happen in their life. This is okay.
   B. You should not say that one child is better than the other in any way. They may be different, but don't let them get the feeling that he or she is better or not as good.

❏ *Acceptance* ❏ *Flexibility*
❏ *Sense of Importance*

● **HELP THE TEENAGER TO PLAN FOR HIS OR HER FUTURE.**

1. Start to talk to the teen about what he or she would like to do (such as jobs, school), where to live, live with someone, marriage, and so on.
2. Wait until you think the teen is able to tell you honestly what goals and dreams he or she has. Then talk about what he or she must do to get ready for this.
3. Together, think of the steps that must be taken; how much and what kind of education, what money is needed and how to get it, how to get to where you need to be, what skills are needed, and so on.

❏ *Responsibility* ❏ *Self-respect* ❏ *Pride*

● **THE TEENAGER SHOULD HELP COOK DINNER ONE NIGHT A WEEK. This helps him or her learn how to live by himself or herself.**

1. Talk about the meal the teen is planning. Is it a balanced meal? Have teen make a list of the things he or she needs for this meal.
2. The teenager should get things ready for dinner and cook it.
   a. You may want to talk about "etiquette", what is the right way to do things, how to set the table, do something that is fun or creative.
   b. The teen may ask you to *help* fix the meal, such as doing something hard, showing him or her how to do something new, and so on.
3. The teen should clean up after dinner. You may want to suggest he or she soaks dishes as they are taken off the table so the food won't stick, and so on.
4. Praise the teen for doing everything that was planned, and so on. "Good meal. I really liked having the break!"

❏ *Approval* ❏ *Trust*
❏ *Responsibility* ❏ *Flexibility*

● **THE TEENAGER SHOULD BE GIVEN SOME MONEY TO BE USED FOR CLOTHES OR THINGS TO TAKE CARE OF THE WAY HE OR SHE LOOKS.**

1. Together, plan how much money is to be spent on clothes and other things, such as deodorant, hair spray, hair cuts, make-up, and so on.

(continued...)

2. Talk about what kind of clothes and hair styles are okay. Both of you need to give your ideas and agree on what is not okay.
3. Talk about how to shop, where to go to shop, when to shop. Does the teen want you to go with him or her when shopping?
4. Praise the teen for his or her choices. If something doesn't fit, talk about how to take it back or get a different size.

   ❏ *Approval* ❏ *Sense of Power* ❏ *Responsibility*
   ❏ *Self-respect* ❏ *Pride* ❏ *Sense of Importance*

● **HELP THE TEENAGER MAKE A PLAN FOR USING THE MONEY HE OR SHE EARNS.**
1. Talk with the teen and together think about what he or she needs and what he or she wants to spend the money on, and how much to *save*.
2. Help the teen to think what is the most important thing to use the money for, the next important thing, and so on.
3. Tell the teen that *gross* pay is *all* the money you get, and *net* pay is how much you have left after you use some for the job, such as car fare, uniforms, taxes, and so on.
4. Help the teen plan a *budget*; how much to spend on needs, wants, entertainment, and savings.
5. If possible, go to the bank with the teen to open a checking and/or a savings account.
6. Show the teen how to write a check, mark it in the book, and balance the check book. You should help the teen until you are sure he or she can do it alone.

   ❏ *Trust* ❏ *Sense of Power* ❏ *Responsibility*
   ❏ *Self-respect* ❏ *Respect for Others*

● *PEER PRESSURE!* **OTHER TEENAGERS OFTEN TRY TO GET HIM OR HER TO DO THINGS, SOME GOOD AND SOME BAD.**
1. Talk together about friends wanting the teen to do something. Think if these are good, bad, or in-between things to do.
2. Talk together about how the teen may want to do something so he or she can be part of a group. Friends may ask the teen to do something, and he or she wants the friends to like him or her.

3. Help the teen think if he or she wants, or doesn't want to do what friends say.
   a. Would I do this on my own, or do it to please my friend?
   b. Is it something that is wrong to do?
   c. How will I feel if I do it? Will I feel guilty that I did the wrong thing?
4. How would you handle it if your friends want you to:
   a. skip school?
   b. take drugs or drink?
   c. destroy someone else's property?
   d. "pick-on" another person (be a bully)?
5. Talk about how the teen can get out of being someplace or doing something that is not right.
   a. Together plan a "code". It can be one word or a few words that means he or she wants you to come and get him or her. "Just called to say "Hello"! ("Hello" may be the *code* word.)
   b. The friends should not know about the "code". This way the teen can use it when he or she needs to get away from the friends.
6. Have the teen say some of the things over and over in front of you so that it will be easy to say it to others, such as "I don't do drugs". Say family rules, such as "I can't do that, I have to be home in ten minutes".
7. Ask the teenager to list "rights and wrongs". If he or she can't, help him or her with the list.
8. Try to get the teen to lead or get his or her friends to do things that are okay. Think before you act!

   ❏ *Sense of Power* ❏ *Self-respect* ❏ *Pride*
● **SHARE THIS WITH YOUR TEENAGER:**
1. You may know the difference between things that are right and things that are wrong to do. Sometimes a friend or group can try to get you to do something you really don't want to do or something that you don't think is right to do, but you don't want them to think that you are afraid or a "chicken". When friends want you to do something you know is bad for you, or something that could get you into trouble...try saying this:
   • "No thanks, I don't do drugs!" or
   • "No thanks, I don't drink!" or
   • "No thanks, I don't want to trash that house!"

   (continued...)

• "You may like the way it makes you feel, but I don't like the way it makes me feel now or later, so I don't want to do it!"

Have the teen try saying this to you so that he or she can hear how it sounds. Then have the teen practice saying this to himself or herself over and over again…so that when put on the spot by a "friend", the teen will know what to say and what it feels like to say it.

❑ *Sense of Power* ❑ *Responsibility*
❑ *Respect for Others* ❑ *Flexibility*

● **TRY TO HAVE FAMILY MEETINGS TO TALK ABOUT THINGS THAT ARE NOT RIGHT, GIVE IDEAS FOR THE FAMILY, THINK WHAT TO DO ABOUT A PROBLEM, OR GIVE PRAISE, AND SO ON.**

1. Have the meetings every week or when some one (any family member) wants a meeting.
2. Each parent should be at the meeting and help to keep it in order.
3. Make some rules:
   a. When can a meeting be called? Anyone in the family should be able to call a meeting.
   b. How long should a meeting last?
   c. Everyone in the family should be at the meeting.
   d. Make rules about the way you should talk, such as no "put-downs", no name calling, and so on.
4. Before the meeting, the parent should meet with each person who has a problem to bring up:
   a. Talk about the problem;
   b. Help the teenager find the right way to present the problem to the group; and
   c. Have the teenager practice the way he or she will talk about the problem with the group.
5. Parents should make sure that everyone has a chance to tell what he or she feels. Then the family should work on a way to help what is wrong, or agree that it cannot be made better.

6. If necessary, tell different ones in the family to do some things to help with a problem.
7. *Always end the meeting with a good feeling. This is very important.*

❑ *Approval* ❑ *Trust*
❑ *Acceptance* ❑ *Sense of Importance*

● **TAKE TIME TO TALK WITH THE TEENAGER ABOUT MANY THINGS.**

1. You can start to talk about something he or she is interested in, such as things happening now in the news, sports, neighborhood, school, and so on.
2. Ask what the teen thinks about something— his or her ideas, feelings, the way he or she might handle something.
3. Try to get the teenager to give ideas by saying something that shows you like what he or she says, such as "You have a good idea" or "I would not have thought of that, that's great!"
4. Ask questions about the teen's ideas. "How would you change situations or things?", "How do you think other kids feel about the situation?"
5. Talk about how you feel and think about something without making the teenager feel you don't like the way he or she thinks (don't be critical). You don't have to agree, but you should respect others' opinions or thoughts.
6. Look at the teenager when you're talking.
7. You can start talking with him or her any time you think of something. It may be while eating, watching TV, listening to music, riding in the car, and so on.
8. You may want to show the teen that it is okay for you not to feel the same way he or she feels by giving a friendly touch on his or her arm or shoulder.
9. End your talk in a good way. "I really like your idea" or "What you said gives me something to think about."

❏ *Approval* ❏ *Trust*
❏ *Acceptance* ❏ *Sense of Importance*

● **TAKE TIME TO TALK WITH THE TEENAGER ABOUT MANY THINGS.**

1. You can start to talk about something he or she is interested in, such as things happening now in the news, sports, neighborhood, school, and so on.

2. Ask what the teen thinks about something— his or her ideas, feelings, the way he or she might handle something.

3. Try to get the teenager to give ideas by saying something that shows you like what he or she says, such as "You have a good idea" or "I would not have thought of that, that's great!"

4. Ask questions about the teen's ideas. "How would you change situations or things?", "How do you think other kids feel about the situation?"

5. Talk about how you feel and think about something without making the teenager feel you don't like the way he or she thinks (don't be critical). You don't have to agree, but you should respect others' opinions or thoughts.

6. Look at the teenager when you're talking.

7. You can start talking with him or her any time you think of something. It may be while eating, watching TV, listening to music, riding in the car, and so on.

8. You may want to show the teen that it is okay for you not to feel the same way he or she feels by giving a friendly touch on his or her arm or shoulder.

9. End your talk in a good way. "I really like your idea" or "What you said gives me something to think about."

❏ *Sense of Power* ❏ *Self-respect* ❏ *Pride*

● **SHARE THIS WITH YOUR TEENAGER:**

1. You may know the difference between things that are right and things that are wrong to do. Sometimes a friend or group can try to get you to do something you really don't want to do or something that you don't think is right to do, but you don't want them to think that you are afraid or a "chicken". When friends want you to do something you know is bad for you, or something that could get you into trouble...try saying this:
   • "No thanks, I don't do drugs!" or
   • "No thanks, I don't drink!" or
   • "No thanks, I don't want to trash that house!"
   • "You may like the way it makes you feel, but I don't like the way it makes me feel now or later, so I don't want to do it!"

   Have the teen try saying this to you so that he or she can hear how it sounds. Then have the teen practice saying this to himself or herself over and over again...so that when put on the spot by a "friend", the teen will know what to say and what it feels like to say it.

❏ *Acceptance* ❏ *Flexibility*
❏ *Sense of Importance*

● **HELP THE TEENAGER TO PLAN FOR HIS OR HER FUTURE.**

1. Start to talk to the teen about what he or she would like to do (such as jobs, school), where to live, live with someone, marriage, and so on.

2. Wait until you think the teen is able to tell you honestly what goals and dreams he or she has. Then talk about what he or she must do to get ready for this.

3. Together, think of the steps that must be taken; how much and what kind of education, what money is needed and how to get it, how to get to where you need to be, what skills are needed, and so on.

**READ CAREFULLY BEFORE YOU
DO THIS EXERCISE WITH THE TEEN
OR GROUP.**

❏ *Trust*

● **FOCUSING ON YOU! GAINING
   CONTROL OF YOURSELF—
   STRESS REDUCING EXERCISE.**

1. Sit straight. Close your eyes or look into your lap. Get comfortable.
2. Tighten your muscles—start at the top of your head—feel the tightness—feel it move down through your hair—down over your eyes— nose—mouth—TIGHTEN—TIGHTEN.
3. Move down your neck—hold tight— count to ten.
4. Let your neck muscle go limp. Let head drop forward slowly—slowly to your chest, then all the way back—as far as you can—feel the muscles—TIGHTEN!
5. Repeat numbers 3 and 4 two more times.
6. Sit quietly—Picture yourself in a very special place where you feel safe and happy. Feel yourself in this place and relax—there's no room for anger there—no place for frustration or stress. Feel the positive flow around you.
7. Just relax—breathe deep—in and out/in and out. Listen to the flow in and flow out—IN goes the positive/OUT the negative. RELAX!
8. Count to ten and open your eyes.
   (Tell the teenager or group that this is a way of focusing on yourself and **taking control of yourself** whenever you may feel frustrated, upset, angry or out of control—you can do it any time, anywhere.)

❏ *Approval* ❏ *Trust*
❏ *Acceptance* ❏ *Sense of Importance*

● **TAKE TIME TO TALK WITH THE TEENAGER ABOUT MANY THINGS.**

1. You can start to talk about something he or she is interested in, such as things happening now in the news, sports, neighborhood, school, and so on.

2. Ask what the teen thinks about something— his or her ideas, feelings, the way he or she might handle something.

3. Try to get the teenager to give ideas by saying something that shows you like what he or she says, such as "You have a good idea" or "I would not have thought of that, that's great!"

4. Ask questions about the teen's ideas. "How would you change situations or things?", "How do you think other kids feel about the situation?"

5. Talk about how you feel and think about something without making the teenager feel you don't like the way he or she thinks (don't be critical). You don't have to agree, but you should respect others' opinions or thoughts.

6. Look at the teenager when you're talking.

7. You can start talking with him or her any time you think of something. It may be while eating, watching TV, listening to music, riding in the car, and so on.

8. You may want to show the teen that it is okay for you not to feel the same way he or she feels by giving a friendly touch on his or her arm or shoulder.

9. End your talk in a good way. "I really like your idea" or "What you said gives me something to think about."

ORDER DIRECT: 1-800-347-BOOK

❑ YES, I want_____copies of
**BASE The Step-By-Step Self-Esteem
Program for Children From Birth to 18**
for $15.95 each plus $2.50 shipping.

❑ Check enclosed for $_____ payable to:
    Westport Publishers • 4050 Pennsylvania Ave.
    Suite 310 • Kansas City, MO 64111
❑ Charge my credit card: ❑ Visa   ❑ MasterCard
    Acct. #_____ Exp. Date _____
    Signature_____

SHIP TO: _____
_____
_____

On BASE! is available at local bookstores.

ORDER DIRECT: 1-800-347-BOOK

❑ YES, I want_____ copies of
**BASE The Step-By-Step Self-Esteem
Program for Children From Birth to 18**
for $15.95 each plus $2.50 shipping.

❑ Check enclosed for $_____ payable to:
    Westport Publishers • 4050 Pennsylvania Ave.
    Suite 310 • Kansas City, MO 64111
❑ Charge my credit card: ❑ Visa   ❑ MasterCard
    Acct. #_____ Exp. Date _____
    Signature_____

SHIP TO: _____
_____
_____

On BASE! is available at local bookstores.